# COLONEL STEPHENS
AND HIS RAILMOTORS

© Brian Janes, Ross Shimmon and Lightmoor Press 2018
Designed by Ian Pope
British Library Cataloguing-in-Publication Data.
A catalogue record for this book is available from the British Library
**ISBN 13: 9781911038 48 1**
All rights reserved. No part of this publication may be reproduced, stored in a retrieval system or transmitted in any form or by any means, electronic, mechanical, photocopying, recording or otherwise, without the written permission of the publisher.

**Lightmoor Press**

Lightmoor Press is an imprint of
Black Dwarf Lightmoor Publications Limited
144b Lydney Industrial Estate, Harbour Road
Lydney, Gloucestershire, GL15 4EJ
Printed in Poland
www.lfbookservices.co.uk

The second Kent & East Sussex Railway's Ford railmotor in the platform at Rolvenden station c.1934. Monty Baker is on the left with Nelson Wood, Harry Simmonds and wife and family.
*CSRM*

# COLONEL STEPHENS AND HIS RAILMOTORS

## BRIAN JANES AND ROSS SHIMMON
### WITH DRAWINGS BY LESLIE DARBYSHIRE

The second K&ESR Ford set showing the low position of the driver compared with the passengers. Another staged photograph apparently using K&ESR staff as passengers.
*CSRM*

## CONTENTS

| | | |
|---|---|---|
| Foreword | | 7 |
| Chapter One | *Gazelle* | 9 |
| Chapter Two | The Kent and East Sussex Railway Pickering Steam Railmotor | 29 |
| Chapter Three | The Weston, Clevedon and Portishead Railway Drewry Railmotors | 43 |
| Chapter Four | The Ford Railmotors and their Direct Ancestor | 63 |
| | The Wolseley-Siddeley | 63 |
| | The Ford Railmotors | 67 |
| | The Kent and East Sussex Railway Set No. 1 | 67 |
| | The Shropshire and Montgomeryshire Set | 74 |
| | Kent and East Sussex Ford Set No. 2 | 78 |
| | The Selsey Tramway Set | 84 |
| | The Colonel's Rail Lorry | 88 |
| | Other Railways | 89 |
| Chapter Five | The Ford Railmotor Experience | 95 |
| Chapter Six | The Shefflex Railmotors | 103 |
| | The Selsey Set | 104 |
| | The Kent and East Sussex Set | 111 |
| Chapter Seven | Incidents and Accidents | 121 |
| Chapter Eight | Railmotor Baggage Trucks | 125 |
| Chapter Nine | Conclusion | 133 |
| Appendix | The Replica Ford Railmotor | 135 |

## INTRODUCTION

In the early 1990s the late Stephen Garrett produced a pioneering work on the history of Colonel Holman Fred Stephens' successful use of railmotors on independent rural light railways. In this he was assisted by the photographic expertise of collector John Scott-Morgan. The book has long been out of print.

Since that publication much research has been undertaken by members of the Colonel Stephens Society and volunteers of the Colonel Stephens Railway Museum on the Kent and East Sussex Railway at Tenterden, who hold an extensive archive on Stephens' Railways. To mark the 150th anniversary of Holman Stephens' birth, the society decided, with the kind permission of the earlier publishers, to extensively revise the earlier work to reflect the research and photographic archive that have been accumulated over the last twenty or so years.

The description 'railmotor' was just one of the terms used to denote self-propelled passenger vehicles, but it was the term most frequently used until the 1930s. Others included 'railmotor cars', 'railmotor omnibuses', 'petrol motor vehicles' and 'petrol railcars'. To avoid confusion we have stuck to 'railmotor'.

This work is, therefore, a combined effort of many people. To the fore have been, naturally, the late Stephen Garrett, together with Albyn Austin, Nigel Bird, Tom Burnham, Laurie Cooksey, Les Darbyshire, Brian Janes, Katie Shimmon, Ross Shimmon and Assistant Archivist of the museum, Bob Clifford.

Hugh Smith
Chairman, Colonel Stephens Society
Philip Shaw
Chairman, Colonel Stephens Railway Museum Committee

# Steam Rail Motor No 6.

Built by Messrs R & Y. Pickering & Co Ltd Wishaw N.B. 1905
Delivered to K & E.S. Railway Coy 3/05

| | |
|---|---|
| Length over Buffers 30'-0" | Width over Body 9'-0" |
| Length over Body 27'-1" | Height from Rail 10'-9" |
| Diameter of Wheels 3'-0" | Size & Length of Journals 8" x 3¾" |
| Total Wheel Base 17'-0" | Seating Accomodation 36 (Third Class only) |

Engine & Boiler for above purchased from Messrs Hutchinson & Co 1904. Dia of Cylinders 5"
New Crank Shaft made by Clarkes Crank & Forge Co Lincoln 1906
Engine thoroughly overhauled & repaired by S.E & C. Rly Coy at their marine works Dover 5/06
New Boiler purchased from Messrs White Bros, Stratford and put in 7/07
New Crank Shaft made by Clarkes Crank & Forge Coy Lincoln and put in 8/08
New Connecting rods made by J. Wright Tipton and put in Feb 1909
New set steel Tubes put in Boiler Aug 1909
New Brass Eccentric Plummer Block Cap put on Aug 1909
Engine & Boiler overhauled March 1910

Engine & Boiler overhauled } May 1911
Tubes, new set
Engine and Boiler overhauled, and fractured stauncheons repaired June 1913
Body left side overhauled and renewed June 1913

**K&ESR Stock Register entry for its Steam Railmotor (see Chapter 2). It gives details of modifications made in an attempt to secure a reliable unit.**  *CSRM*

# FOREWORD

Holman Fred Stephens, later known as Colonel Stephens following a long and distinguished period of Territorial Army Service, was born on the 15th November 1868. He gained a widespread reputation as an accomplished manager and engineer to a collection of independent standard and narrow-gauge railways. Stephens had been associated with some of these railways since the planning stage, whilst others had benefited from his advice once they were up and running. He was also involved with the engineering and construction of a number of other railways on which he held no subsequent management role, and with the planning and promotion of railways for which authority was refused, or that failed to attract sufficient investment.

The railways associated with Stephens were quite separate concerns, but had many features in common. Most were built under the Light Railways Act 1896, or subsequently brought within the provisions of that act, which allowed railways to be built and operated to less exacting standards than those to be found on the main lines. Stephens' railways were therefore cheaply built and cheaply run. When the capital was available, new stock was bought, but frequently this was achieved by the purchase of second-hand equipment. As the 20th century progressed, his railways became famous as living museums of rolling stock, signalling and track that had been discarded by the larger railway companies.

Holman Stephens passionately believed in light railways to serve the needs of rural communities, and that their success relied on them being built and run at low cost. However, even the smallest conventional steam engines were expensive to buy and run. On building his first independent railway, the Rye and Camber, Stephens expressed a wish to use a railmotor. His first connection with this form of propulsion seems to have been his proposal of a Hornsby-Ackroyd compression-ignited oil locomotive for operating the narrow-gauge Rye and Camber Tramway. This was a step too far for the technology of the day, and the tramway opened in 1895 with steam locomotives.

Ten years later he returned with another innovation: a light steam railmotor. Unfortunately, it proved mechanically unreliable, and increasing traffic and the First World War brought the experiment to an end.

Stephens was no antiquarian. He was an early member of the Royal Flying Club and an enthusiastic motorist, and was happy to seek out and employ new ideas on his railways if they offered economies in operation with minimal capital outlay. His railways were pioneers in the use of concrete for the construction of bridges and sleepers, but it was his early use of internal combustion vehicles for which he is perhaps best remembered as an innovator. During the First World War, petrol road-lorry and bus development leapt forward, and traffic on rural railways was under threat. To help counter this, Stephens turned again to the new technology.

He eventually obtained a small petrol locomotive for the Camber Tramway in 1924. He also experimented, with varying degrees of success, with a selection of small internal combustion shunters on the Festiniog and Welsh Highland Railways, plus two adapted Fordson tractors for the Weston, Clevedon and Portishead Railway. However, Stephens does not appear to have attempted to acquire petrol or diesel locomotives for his standard gauge railways, perhaps because they were too expensive and underdeveloped at the time to haul the necessary loads at the, admittedly slow, schedules required. He was, however, a pioneer of the use of light passenger-carrying railmotors, and made extensive use of petrol railmotors on his railways. These and the steam railmotors that preceded them, are the subject of this book.

The first use of a petrol vehicle was in October 1921 on the WC&PR, but the vehicles proved too expensive to adopt on cash-starved independent light railways. Stephens, therefore, turned to adapted road vehicles to meet his needs and had good cause to be pleased with the modifications in the early days. Capital costs were low; reliability and high daily mileages seemed possible – and, indeed, this proved to be the case. Average petrol consumption was very good and other costs would also have been favourable. One member of the crew was saved and, with no engine preparation needed, overtime was, no doubt, cut on locomotive preparation. Stephens was always enthusiastic about the development of these railmotors, although he designated them experimental. However, they were regarded by the operating staff with some trepidation as their mechanical shortcomings were a constant source of difficulty. Economies were achieved, but the service was augmented. If, as a result, passenger comfort was compromised, it was probably no worse than that on the contemporary competing road-bus services.

Rapid road-vehicle development soon changed this dramatically, and bus technology improved by leaps and bounds, leaving the railmotors technically obsolescent well before the end of the 1920s. Nevertheless, lack of capital for replacements delayed their final withdrawal from service until the late 1930s.

*Gazelle* in the locomotive yard at King's Lynn after its epic return trip from King's Lynn to Chesterfield on the 25th July 1897. *CSRM*

The interest sparked by the advertisement led to the publication of a short, illustrated description of *Gazelle*, with some details of the Chesterfield trip, in the May 1901 issue of the Locomotive Magazine, but no sale resulted, which surely didn't come as too much of a surprise.

William Burkitt himself died at the age of 81 on the 7th June 1906, and, in 1909, the locomotive was sold to the machinery and scrap dealer Thos. W. Ward & Co. of the Albion Works, Sheffield. They advertised her for sale in January 1910, and Holman Stephens probably purchased the locomotive in the Autumn of that year for use as an inspection engine during reconstruction work on the Shropshire and Montgomeryshire Light Railway. She was in more or less her original condition, but soon a small temporary windshield was fitted and she was painted in an unlined green or, less likely, black livery. Numbered '1' on arrival on the S&MR, she does not appear to have carried the number for many years.

Once the line between Shrewsbury and Llanymynech had been opened to traffic in April 1911, and her inspection duties on the Criggion Branch were completed, she was used for service trains on that branch. When it was reopened for goods traffic in February 1912 and for passengers in August 1912, she became, in effect, a railmotor as an economical machine for the very light passenger traffic. A more frequent service became possible, compared with the otherwise solitary mixed train, which was all that was needed for the quarry and other goods traffic on offer at that time. Initially, this may have been in her inspection engine form, as it was probably the open cab that prompted complaints by the vicar of Criggion, Reverend R. Brock, whose letter dated the 23rd November 1912 to the Board of Trade read:

I booked today my fare by the 3.57 train from Abbey Gate station to Criggion on the Shropshire & Montgomeryshire Rly. I rode to Kinnerley Junction by a properly equipped train. Proceeding to the branch to Criggion, I was put with another man and two women into the back part of an engine with only a screen between us and the fire – no roof and the sparks and smuts falling over us – one spark nearly got into my eye – with danger of being blinded – my clothes too injured by the same. I wish to know whether passengers can thus be treated and deceived – for the last time I came about a fortnight ago I was conveyed in a carriage

Photographed after arrival on the Shropshire & Montgomeryshire Railway in 1910 *Gazelle* is seen on Kinnerley shed. Note there is still no protection at all for the driver. T. R. Perkins, a well-known railway enthusiast, is believed to be on the footplate. By 1932 Perkins had managed to travel over all passenger carrying lines in the British Isles. CSRM

Taken soon after *Gazelle*'s arrival on the S&MR at Kinnerley shed in 1910. Note the small windshield has been added as the only protection for the driver. *CSRM*

*Gazelle* undertaking her inspection duties during reconstruction of the former Potteries, Shrewsbury & North Wales Railway to form the Shropshire & Montgomeryshire Railway's Criggion branch. *CSRM*

as I have hitherto been. I have had occasion to use the Rly for my wife and daughter and friends from London and of course I cannot subject them to such risk and barbarous treatment.

If they cannot or will not serve proper accommodations through the journey, they should not be allowed to advertise it – there were carriages at the station [Kinnerley] and as an engine ran – a carriage could and should have been on the back.

Stephens replied to the Board of Trade explaining the situation:

I reply to your communication of 30th November and find that it is usual, owing to the slight traffic on the branch in question, to utilise the services of the inspection engine for the afternoon train as the occasion arises. Wind screens are provided and in view of the smallness of the traffic it is considered that the action is justifiable.

W. F. Marwood writing on behalf of the Board of Trade, did not agree:

I am to state for the information of your directors that it is considered that a proper carriage for the conveyance of passengers should be run on the train in question.

The Board of Trade's recommendation (they could not instruct the company) can hardly be considered as ambiguous, but Stephens was not easily put off. At about this time, *Gazelle* acquired a small wooden shelter over the seating area, which had all the welcome appearance of a portable prison cell, with two forward-facing 'porthole' windows and square windows on either side of the rear door. It was eventually completed with luggage rails on the curved roof a foot, or more, shorter than the driver's cab, presumably to improve the driver's vision when running in reverse. The original half-height rear door was retained, but the rest of the doorway remained open to the elements. Baggage could be carried on the roof, which was surrounded by an incongruously ornamental pair of luggage rails.

More extensive changes soon followed, for at some time before July 1913, she was converted into an 0-4-2WT so that she was better able to haul a horse tramcar that had now been acquired to run with her as a trailer. Technically she now ceased to be a railmotor, but the tramcar conversion was inextricably linked to her due to their common non-standard buffing heights.

*Gazelle's* conversion was almost certainly undertaken at Kinnerley (rather than at the oft reported Bagnall works at Stafford) over the 1912/13 winter, for she was first shown as an 0-4-2 in the 1913 statutory

After conversion to an 0-4-2WT, *Gazelle*, now with the shelter over the seating area, is seen at Kinnerley Junction. The 'Terrier' in the background looks large by comparison. *CSRM*

This detail shows the elegant curved brass plate showing *Gazelle*'s name and construction details and the oval ownership plate, common to many of the Stephens' railways, added on conversion from 2-2-2WT. *CSRM*

returns. As can be seen on the locomotive today, this reconstruction was quite simple, if ingenious. It involved substituting the original driving wheels for new cast-iron ones of the same diameter as the leading and trailing wheels, one of which was used as a pattern for the new drivers. Apart from the new connecting rods and new patch plates on the motion plate, the only other changes were minor ones to brake hangers, springs etc. However, the locomotive's looks were not improved as the large driving wheel splashers were retained. Dwarfing the tiny boiler, a very basic cab (with only front and side sheets) was added at the same time, which increased the height of the engine by around six inches, and at a slightly later date a tall and elegant hooter whistle, apparently similar to that fitted to Stephens' 1906 K&ESR steam railmotor, raised the height even further. An oval brass plate on each splasher was added at this time, bearing the legend 'Shropshire and Montgomeryshire Railway Company'. Any original elegance was lost in these unconnected visual changes and additions.

The tramcar had started life as a double-deck two-horse vehicle, which had been designed and built by the North Metropolitan Tramways at its Union Road Works in Leytonstone, London, sometime between 1885 and 1899. It boasted seven tall windows, with fixed top-lights on either side of its lower deck and the clerestory roof had ventilator lights. In typical tramcar

A London County Council horse tram, in original condition, of a similar type to the one converted to *Gazelle*'s trailer. *CSRM*

*Gazelle* with its first trailer, the former London double-deck tramcar, showing original SMR lettering. *CSRM*

fashion, downstairs, a longitudinal wooden seat for eleven passengers ran along each side facing inwards, whilst accommodation on the upper deck for twenty-four passengers was provided on two rows of six wooden 'garden seats' with reversible backs on either side of the central gangway. A centrally positioned arched door slid internally to the right to provide access to the lower saloon from the platforms at either end, and curved staircases led up to the open upper deck. Unladen weight, in original condition, was about

Interior view of the former tramcar trailer, showing relatively luxurious seating of buttoned cushions and decorated plywood seatbacks. Through the sliding end door is the arresting sight of *Gazelle*'s smokebox. *H. J. Stretton Ward (Elro/R. P. Hendry collection)*

two tons. This vehicle is recorded as having arrived on the railway in October 1911, but it languished at Kinnerley for about twelve months before being despatched to the Midland Wagon Works, adjacent to Abbey Station, Shrewsbury, where it was extensively modified. The work involved discarding the top deck and stairs, strengthening the underframe and adding tiny sprung round buffers at either end. With the end platforms also removed, access to the vehicle was only possible via a step below and between the buffers from between the running lines; the foot plate was in two parts to allow the coupling to pass between each section to join up with *Gazelle*. A vertically mounted four-spoked brake wheel at waist level on the outside of each end bulkhead worked the brakes via chains, and on the same side as these wheels. There was a large lamp-housing above the shortened end window. In this condition, the vehicle was approximately 13ft long and 6ft 6in. wide with wheels 1ft 6in. in diameter. The interior still had longitudinal seats in pierced plywood, but the seats were blessed with buttoned cushions. In an overall blue livery, to begin with, (possibly) red painted letters, shaded in white, proudly displayed the characters 'S. & M. R.' centrally on either side, with 'N⁰ 16.' at the right-hand end. The letters and numbers were later replaced with individual smaller yellow metal ones, screwed on immediately below the waist line. It was reportedly the last job undertaken in the Shrewsbury works before they were closed and removed to Birmingham in late 1912. The resultant carriage was probably ex-works in June 1912.

*Gazelle* continued to regularly work the Criggion Branch, and to be used by Stephens for inspection and occasional pleasure trips. From Autumn 1928, passenger services on the Criggion Branch were reduced to Saturdays only and she was probably laid aside. By May 1932, *Gazelle* was stripped down on the 'dump' siding behind the water tower at Kinnerley.

In 1936, the decision was taken to restore the diminutive locomotive for use, once more, as an inspection and light-traffic engine, probably as a result of the demise of the S&MR's railmotor. The work was carried out by the company's fitter-in-charge, Mr Charlie Owen, in the workshops at Kinnerley. In June 1937, the engine emerged, phoenix-like from the shed, complete with new chimney, in a smart olive-green livery, lined with broad black bands, edged in white, with vermilion buffer beams, connecting rods and guard-irons, and brown main frames. Her wooden shelter was also rebuilt and refitted in a slightly modified form, now extending slightly more over the side sheets and without the roof railings, which had disappeared some years before.

*Gazelle* on Criggion Branch duty at Kinnerley Junction. Note the tall whistle on the cab roof and the luggage railings still in place. *CSRM*

*Gazelle* in Kinnerley yard running bunker first with the former London tramcar trailer. *CSRM*

The locomotive stripped down behind the water tower at Kinnerley Junction. This view shows the method of entry to the original passenger shelter. *CSRM*

Stripped down a little further with the refurbished boiler in place.  *CSRM*

In June 1937, the engine emerged, phoenix-like from the shed, in smart olive-green livery, lined with broad black bands, edged in white.  *CSRM*

*Gazelle* with rebuilt trailer formed from the former Wolseley-Siddeley railmotor body mounted on the former London horse tramcar underframe.  
*CSRM*

To accompany her, the tramcar was rebuilt. Its body was removed from its chassis and it took up a position beside the siding, mounted on four oil drums and two lengths of timber. Next, the body of the ex-Wolseley-Siddeley railmotor body was renovated and placed on the chassis. Reversible wooden seats were installed, most probably from one of the Ford railmotors, for up to twenty passengers. Also adapted to run with *Gazelle*, the previously infrequently used petrol railmotor goods truck was modified with the necessary low-level miniature buffers.

On the 6th February 1941, the War Department made an inventory showing the condition of all of the S&MR locomotives, and it had this to report regarding *Gazelle*:

> Firebox and smokebox fair, wheels beginning to wear, side rod bushes wearing, play in eccentric straps and quadrant block, big end brasses wearing, but general condition good. Tools consisted of 1 shovel, 1 rake and 1 pricker, all of which were serviceable.

Minus the wooden passenger shelter, which was considered to obstruct the view, plenty of work was found for her as an early morning inspection unit when sabotage was suspected. She also found work as a VIP carrier until the carriage chassis reportedly broke in two. She was used unofficially as convenient transport to pubs on the Criggion Branch, and last officially steamed on the 7th April 1942, being taken out of service when the army's Wickham petrol trolleys took over her work. Then she was stored in various open-air locations around the Kinnerley

The previously little-used baggage trailer intended to work with the petrol railmotors was adapted to work with *Gazelle*.  
*CSRM*

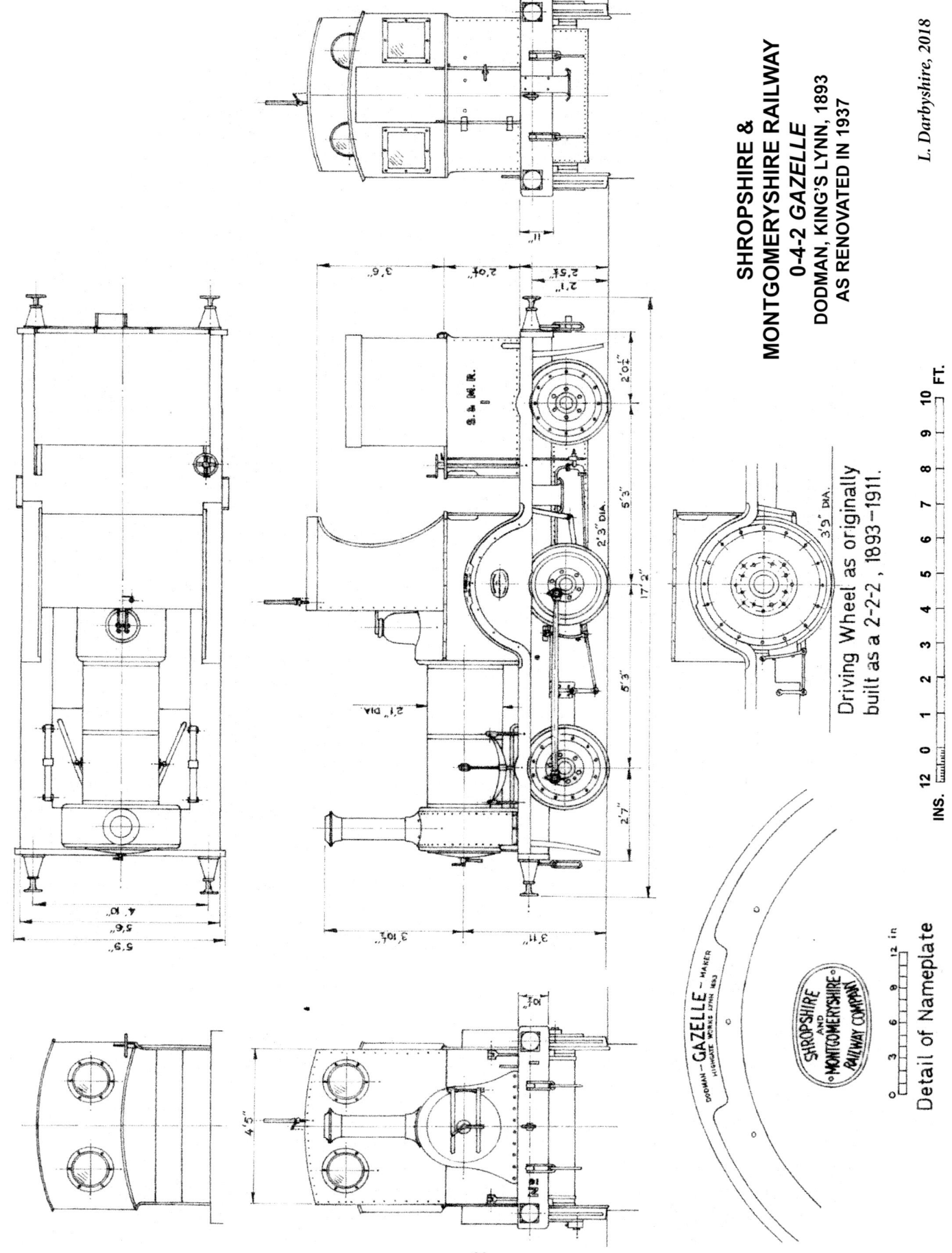

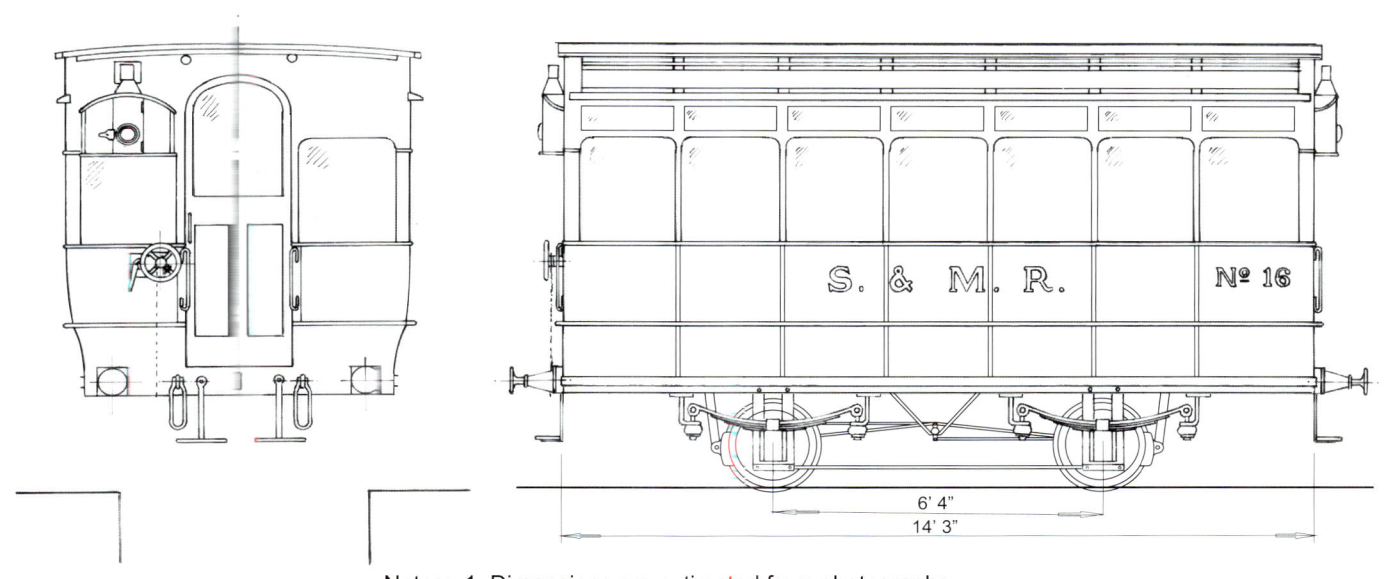

**SHROPSHIRE & MONTGOMERYSHIRE RAILWAY**
*GAZELLE'S* ORIGINAL TRAILER 1911–c1939
Ex- L.C.C. HORSE TRAM CAR

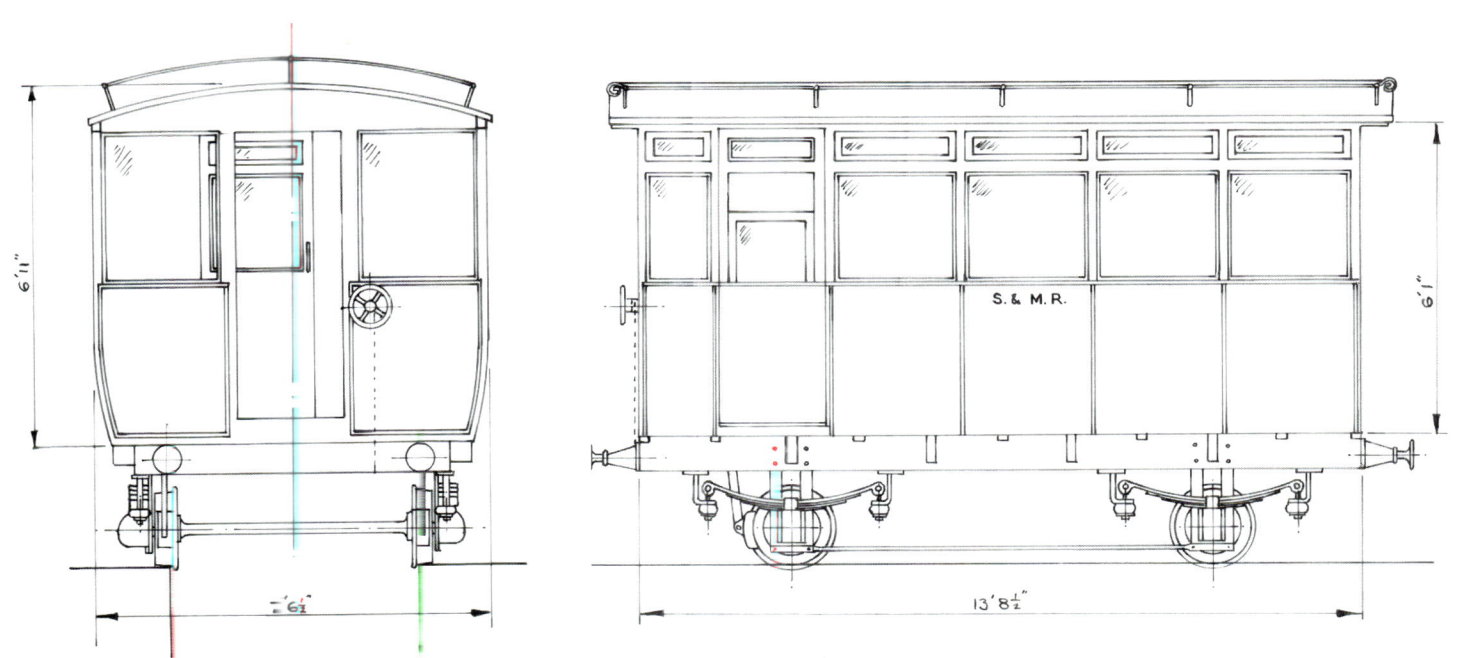

**SHROPSHIRE & MONTGOMERYSHIRE RAILWAY**
*GAZELLE'S* LATER TRAILER c1939
Ex- WOLSELEY-SIDDELEY RAILMOTOR

L. Darbyshire, 2018

*Gazelle* in Kinnerley shed with the trailer formed from the Wolseley-Siddeley railmotor body and the tramcar underframe.
*CSRM*

*Gazelle,* probably on an excursion. *CSRM*

This angle demonstrates how small *Gazelle* is compared with its trailer. Note the decorative flourish to the railings around the luggage rack. *CSRM*

site where, at some time, a War Department ex-GWR 0-6-0 'Dean' goods locomotive accidentally ran into her, damaging the rear of the passenger compartment and its door (subsequently welded shut). She had already lost her chimney on a trip to Criggion, probably through corrosion; the stump had been replaced with a piece of cast-iron pipe. She was, nevertheless, cared for in a casual sort of way and repainted whilst in store in a colour variously described as 'pea green' and 'light grey'.

Along with the surviving S&MR engines, *Gazelle* was officially taken over at nationalization. C. H. Calder, the Operating Officer, held the engine in great affection and he seems to have been instrumental in securing her for the future. The army cosmetically restored and repainted her in plain dark-green livery, relieved by a black boiler band and garish red footplate valences and coupling rods. Still minus the passenger shelter (which remained dumped at Kinnerley in the immediate post-war period), and with a crude solid wooden lip top affixed to her cast-iron pipe chimney, she was moved to the Longmoor Military Railway in

Head-on photograph of *Gazelle*, again probably taken on an excursion. *CSRM*

The slightly wider wooden shelter is clearly shown here. Plenty of youthful interest surrounding *Gazelle* during what must be an excursion, with school uniforms well in evidence. *CSRM*

A Birmingham Locomotive Club excursion in April 1938, behind *Gazelle* at Llanymynech. *CSRM*

Awaiting participants on a Birmingham Locomotive Society excursion in April 1938. Note the difference in height between the platform and the footplate. *CSRM*

*Gazelle* minus the wooden passenger shelter. She was cared for in a casual sort of way, repainted in a colour variously described as 'pea green' and 'light grey'. Note too, the replacement chimney. *CSRM*

**Little and large!** *Gazelle* in front of *Gordon* at a Longmoor open day. *CSRM*

**Repainted into S&M livery and mounted on a length of rail at Longmoor.** *courtesy Mike Christensen*

*Gazelle* at the Museum of Army Transport at Beverley in Yorkshire. *Official Postcard*

Hampshire, and attended their open day on the 3rd September 1949.

Thus it was that when the Western Region of British Railways formally withdrew *Gazelle* from stock in the summer of 1950, she yet again escaped the scrap man's torch. Sir Eustace Missenden of the Railway Executive Committee, wrote on the 4th August 1950 to the Director of Transport at the War Office, Brigadier R. Gardiner, offering the engine for preservation in the War Department Museum at Longmoor. *Gazelle* was soon afterwards put on display on a short length of track on the parade ground there and cared for by the army for many years, being painted much later in Longmoor's standard blue livery.

When Longmoor closed in 1970, the locomotive was put on display at the National Railway Museum, before moving to the Museum of Army Transport at Beverley in Yorkshire in 1981. At the beginning of 1997, that museum also closed and *Gazelle* was moved to the newly opened Colonel Stephens Railway Museum at Tenterden, on the K&ESR, where, on long-term loan, he enjoys pride of place as the only S&MR locomotive to survive, repainted in her 1937 livery with a suitable replacement chimney.

*Gazelle* being prepared for its journey from the Colonel Stephens Railway Museum at Tenterden, Kent to the Railfest exhibition at the National Railway Museum, York in 2012. *Gazelle* remains on long-term loan from the NRM to the Tenterden museum. Note the newly-applied, correct, Shropshire & Montgomeryshire Railway livery and the replica of the original chimney. *Brian Janes*

The K&ESR Pickering steam railmotor pictured at the Pickering works at Wishaw in 1905 before delivery. It was a basic example of the Edwardian coachbuilder's art. Numbered 16 in the railway's carriage stock list, it is carrying the standard early K&ESR livery of ivory and brown. The suspension is basic and the water tank, hanging from the central underframe made for poor weight distribution and looks vulnerable to damage.

*R. Y. Pickering/CSRM*

# – CHAPTER 2 –

# THE KENT AND EAST SUSSEX RAILWAY'S PICKERING STEAM RAILMOTOR

Interesting as she was, *Gazelle* had been adapted from an existing older locomotive. Holman Stephens' first example of a self-propelled passenger-carrying vehicle was a newly designed and built steam railmotor purchased in 1905 for the Kent & East Sussex Railway (K&ESR). In that year, the railway technical press was filled with the latest development in economical transport – the newly minted term, 'railmotor'. The *Locomotive Magazine* in that year carried news of a new railcar every month, but most of these were bogie carriages with a small engine conventionally built on the same chassis. Originally envisaged to increase frequency and reduce costs on routes that competed with the then current arch enemy – the electric tram – there were exceptions. Tucked away at the end of an article on the latest batch of railmotors in the *Locomotive Magazine* of March 1905, there was a description of an experimental machine designed to be used on rural light railways. She was very different from all the others: a 4-wheeled machine owing far more to road steam lorry practice than the blending of conventional locomotives and carriages that the others represented. Stephens was again innovating to try to keep down the cost of operating a rural light railway, and the K&ESR acquired its sixth item of motive power when delivery was effected in early 1905.

The railmotor craze had started a year or two earlier. Soon after his appointment as General Manager of the London & South Western Railway (L&SWR), Sir Charles Owens came to the conclusion that material economies might be achieved by running a powered single coach. The resultant design, produced at Nine Elms Works, began regular working in June 1903. Even before this, the Great Western Railway asked to copy the design. This was agreed, and the GWR made the very sensible decision to substantially enlarge the boiler unit. Both railways immediately claimed a very appreciable reduction in the cost of haulage, without the withdrawal of any accommodation required by the public. The other railways poured out designs over the next three years, with very mixed success. Some persisted and met with modest success, continuing services until the First World War, but others quickly succumbed to poor performance and/or passenger discomfort. Only the GWR and the Lancashire & Yorkshire persisted beyond this.

Matching the railmotor craze at this time was the enthusiasm on the road for the steam lorry, and, in particular, the then modern relatively lightweight 'undertype' lorry with high-speed geared engines and vertical boilers. Historic trials in Liverpool in 1899 and 1901 had proved the economy and practicability of the steam lorry, and a seminal book published in 1906 claimed:

During the past fifteen years considerable progress has been made in high-speed engines, and reliable data are now available which prove beyond all doubt that this class of engine can be relied on – prophecies to the contrary notwithstanding – and that greater signs of wear in a given period are not more observable than in ordinary slow-running engines. The advantages of 'high speed' (in economical use of steam and power/weight ratio) are practically acknowledged by the majority of makers who run their engines as fast as they consider prudent.

The Sentinel lorry of the period had a classic undertype configuration with a compact tube boiler mounted ahead of the front axle, an engine having cylinders with 6in. bore and 10in. stroke slung amidships under the framing. It attained engine speeds of 300 revolutions per minute, geared down through a chain drive to the rear wheels. Such speeds allowed a far more lightweight unit than railway locomotive-type mechanisms, but they tended to be more complicated and needed sophisticated gearing and lubrication, with all the moving parts running in a bath of oil.

There was another problem too. The early years of the twentieth century saw many makes of undertype steam wagons come and go, and, with hindsight, all of them suffered from inefficient boilers. Many went well enough when supplied with sufficient steam, but on hills they stalled because of the inability of their boilers to produce the required volume of steam quickly enough. Locomotive-type boilers came back into fashion and weights increased until Sentinel perfected its designs in the early 1920s and the lighter vertical boiler made its come back. The undertype could be a difficult wagon to design and maintain, but it had one great point in its favour: if the failings in boiler design were cured, its compact design took up very little load space.

This view of the cab interior shows a classic steam launch cylinder unit, mounted transversely on the right-hand side, supplied by an equally classic launch-type vertical boiler on the left, driving a centrally mounted chain-geared drive. *CSRM*

A 'Standard' Sentinel steam lorry.  *Ian Pope collection*

Stephens, with his advocacy of a modern and cost-effective approach to rural transport, would have been very aware of all these developments and he must have wished to try them out. He was actively involved in the design of the new railcar and took a particularly proprietorial attitude to it when it appeared. The firm he chose to build the carriage portion was his current favourite, R. Y. Pickering & Co. Ltd of Wishaw, near Glasgow, who were predominantly wagon and carriage builders with no knowledge or experience of steam machinery.

The first mention of a railcar in Pickering's records is an enquiry sent on the 22nd February 1904, and received on the 23rd February, for a quotation from Messrs Rother Valley Rly Co. Tonbridge and was for a single 6-wheeled motor carriage. They replied on the 9th March 1904 and, under Order 7647, proposed a steam motor carriage: *We to try to build @ £75 Engine & £225 carriage portion. Price received £395.* The order was finalised with the newly renamed Kent and East Sussex Railway on the 8th August 1904, noting that *they to supply Engine and Boiler.* The order states:

Build One Steam Motor Carriage Complete to Our Drawing Nos. [blank]. They supply Engine & Boiler. Reynolds Patent Silent Driving Chain, etc, 14ft - 0in. Wheel Base. 24ft - 0in. Long Over Headstocks. Third Class. Smoker & Guards (sic) Compartment. Painting etc. – Particulars later. Painted No. 16. D/l F.O.C delivered free of charge) at [blank]. D/y in August. To Order of Kent & East Sussex Rly. Tonbridge.

The new railcar's mechanism had been purchased separately from Hutchinson & Company some months before the railcar was delivered. Hutchinson & Co. was not a lorry or crane manufacturer, although there was a Hutchison & Company, Boilermakers, at 25 Mair Street, Glasgow in the 1905 Glasgow trade directory. Sadly, a more detailed specification, or any plans, do not seem to have survived. Pickering's Stores Day Book, dated the 10th February 1905, records that *one new steam motor carriage complete was sent to Robertsbridge that day, carriage paid*, but it appears the steam railmotor was not complete, as the same book, page 430, just twelve days later, advises that *one sprocket wheel 32T and 1 chain 9ft 9in. x 4* was forwarded to H. F. Stephens Esq. at Tonbridge. On the 8th March 1905, *two screw couplings and balls (for motor car)* were also sent down by rail to Robertsbridge. Having only been fitted originally with a three-link coupling at either end (for emergency use), these new couplings were possibly to enable the railmotor to tow a wagon and thus become a little more versatile.

The K&ESR loco register records:

### Steam railmotor No. 6
Built by Messrs R. & Y. Pickering & Co. Ltd, Wishaw. M.B. 1905
Delivered to K&ES Railway Coy 3/05
Length over buffers       30ft 0in.
Width over Body          9ft 0in.
Length over Body         27ft 1in.
Height from Rail          10ft 9in.

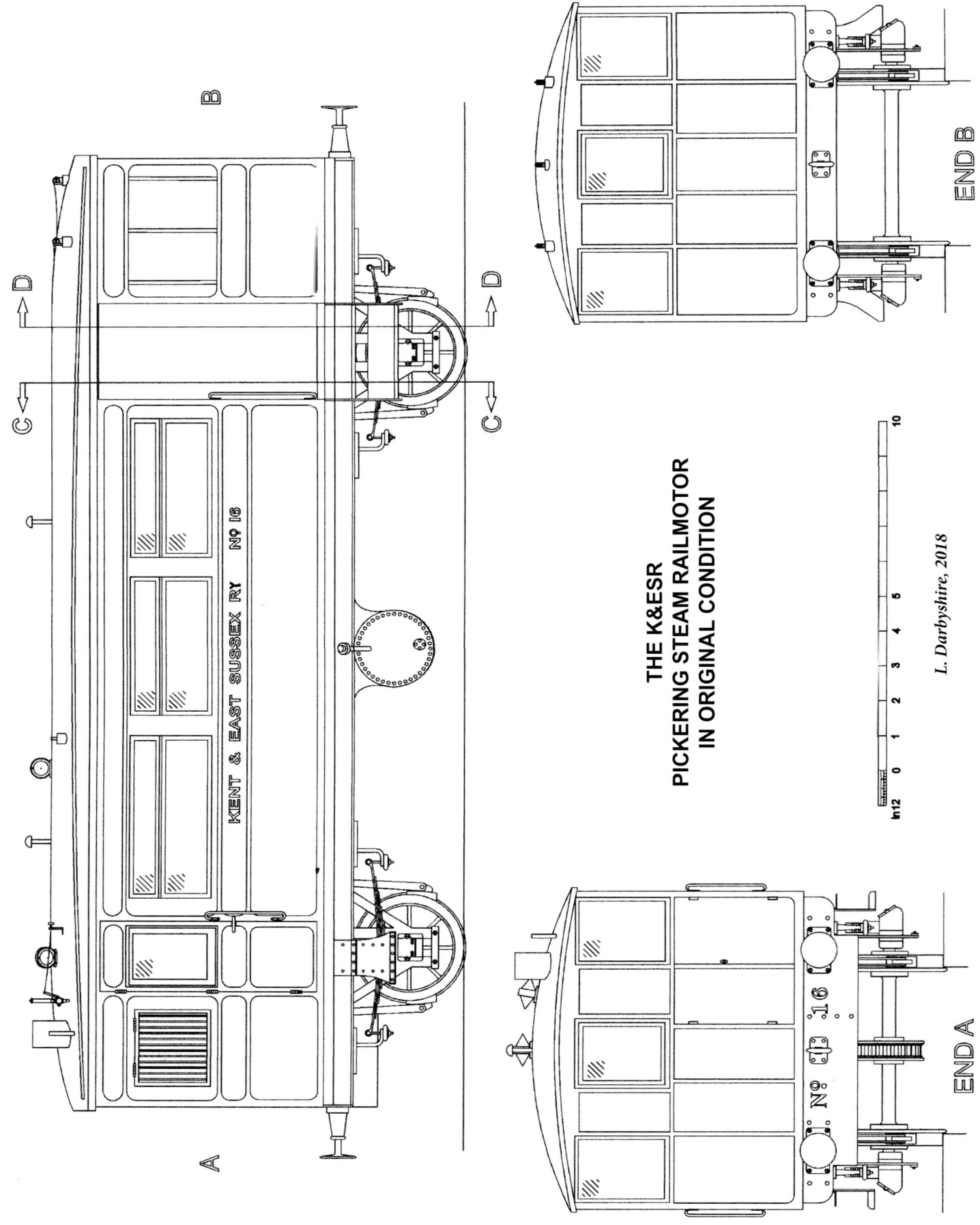

Diameter of Wheels 3ft 0in.
Total Wheel Base 17ft 0in.
Seating Accommodation 36 (Third Class only)
Engine & Boiler for above purchased from Messrs Hutchinson & Co. 1904
Dia. of Cylinders 5in.

This record shows notable enlargements of length and wheelbase from the original order, which may reflect Stephens' original wish for a 6-wheeler. Unfortunately, we have virtually no record of the mechanical components of the railmotor; we only have the bare details and a photograph of the interior to guide us. It had a pair of 5½ in. (5in. in K&ESR records) cylinders with ordinary (Stephenson) link motion, supplied with steam by a vertical multitubular boiler and driving a layshaft connected by Reynolds Patent Silent Drive Chain to the nearest axle. Later, secondary sources claim a piston stroke of 9in., a boiler 2ft 0in. diameter by 5ft, working to a relatively low pressure of 140lbs. The photograph of the cab interior shows a classic steam launch cylinder unit mounted transversely on the right-hand side, supplied by an equally classic launch-type vertical boiler on the left, driving a centrally mounted chain-geared drive.

Although these basic units were far from modern by contemporary road-design standards, and may have even been second-hand, as a whole, the railmotor was set up with considerable affinity to steam-lorry style, with a relatively high-speed unit that had gearing and boiler mounted at the front on the left-hand side. Amidships it carried a small quantity of water (quoted later as 150 gallons, perhaps enough for ten miles) to counter-balance the weight of the power unit. However, it must be doubted that this

The front of the engine compartment was divided into five vertical panels and painted in one dark colour, probably brown but possibly red. *CSRM*

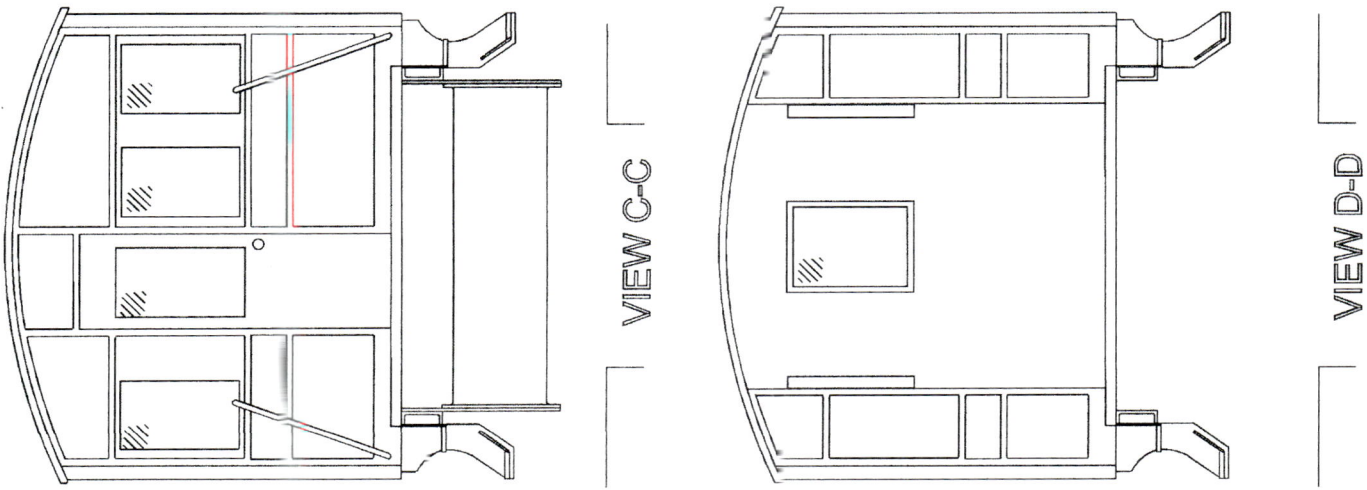

was a satisfactory distribution of weight. Without a decent load in the passenger accommodation, this distribution would have resulted in a very bouncy ride, which would have worsened as the water was used up. In addition, there would probably have been an imbalance between the weight of the boiler on one side and the other cab machinery. An underslung lorry unit between the wheels would have vastly improved the weight distribution and consequent ride. Stephens' railmotor seems to have been doomed from the design stage, and a picture emerges of a vehicle trying to tear itself apart as it progressed along the line.

Photographs do survive of the railmotor at Pickering's works prior to delivery. These show that it was painted in the railway's brown and ivory livery, with a narrow ivory waist panel lettered 'KENT & EAST SUSSEX RY No. 16'. The railcar body itself was a basic example of the Edwardian coachbuilder's art. The front of the engine compartment was divided into five vertical panels and painted in one dark colour, probably brown but possibly red. The upper sections of the outer and centre panels were glazed. Neither the end nor sides of the engine compartment had any apparent doorway or hatch large enough to remove the boiler for attention. Hook couplings with chains were provided at either end, but were probably intended for towing the railmotor rather than for attaching wagons or other stock to be pulled by it. It looked handsome enough, but like the later petrol railmotors, passenger comfort was minimal to non-existent. Adjoining the engine room was, logically, a smoking compartment with eleven seats, then a non-smoking compartment for twenty, and after that an intermediate vestibule open to the elements on both sides, and finally a guard's compartment claimed to seat six and stand four, with twelve to fourteen milk churns and baggage. This all seems a little improbable in the space provided and, if ever loaded like this on market days, it would have put modern tube travel in perspective. The guard's compartment also contained basic driving controls, with a form of steam shut-off, a whistle cord and a gong to signal the driver. It is probable that when running with the guard's end forward, controls were operated by a three-wire wire-and-pulley system rather similar to that used on L&SWR push-and-pull vehicles. There were wires going rearwards from the driving end from brackets with pulleys on them. At the guard's end there were three sets of pulleys supported by brackets on cylindrical 'pots'. It is thought that the wires operated the whistle and the other two were joined to the ends of the regulator handle.

Clearly based on a press release from Stephens himself, the *Transport & Railway Gazette*, dated the 23rd June 1905, advised:

**Stephens-Pickering Rail Autocar**
(We here illustrate) a steam rail Autocar which was built to the designs of Mr. H. F. Stephens, Managing Director of the Kent & East Sussex Railway, by R. Y. Pickering & Co., Limited, of Wishaw.

To secure economy in working the car has been constructed in as light a manner as possible consistent with the work it has to do. It has also been made as wide as possible to give the utmost possible accommodation in the length, which is only 27 ft.

There is accommodation, in ordinary circumstances, for 31 passengers. For an unusual rush of passengers the luggage compartment can be utilised for their accommodation, as it is provided with folding seats, and can accommodate 10 extra people. In ordinary working this luggage compartment has accommodation for the ordinary parcel traffic and passengers' luggage.

The car is driven by a pair of engines with 5½ in. cylinders, supplied by steam from a multitubular boiler. Steam can be shut off and the brake applied and the whistle blown from either end of the car.

The steam railmotor clearly lived up to its experimental label. High engine speeds stressed the crankshaft and two new ones were made in the first three years. The new crankshaft had to be made for the railmotor by Clarke's Crank & Forge Co. of Lincoln in 1906, after which the K&ESR's Rolling Stock Ledger records the following repairs:

May, 1906: Engine thoroughly overhauled and repaired by the South Eastern & Chatham Railway at their marine works, Dover.
August, 1908: Another new crank shaft supplied by Clarke's Crank & Forge Co. of Lincoln and put in.

These problems initiated enquiries of Pickering in January 1906 for a new marine engine, and Stephens also enquired about buying two motor car engines at about £25 each or *marine engines (steam?) suitable for a motor car*. In May, he was offered two suitable engines at £78 each, repaired and delivered, but the option was not taken up. Were the motor car engines internal combustion engines, and was Stephens again demonstrating the same fascination for the new technology that he had displayed on the Rye & Camber? We do not know, but for certain the Hutchinson boiler was shown as inadequate and, after only two years, it was replaced, in July 1907, by a new and considerably larger one from White Bros, Stratford. The London trade directory for 1907 lists a White Brothers, Engineers and Machinery Merchants, Princes Wharf, High Street, Stratford, East London, but no further details are known. It seems likely that this boiler was secondhand.

The boiler change and associated work seems to have changed the appearance of the vehicle in several ways. The chimney was shortened and a large safety valve appeared on the roof to join the already prominent hooter. Incidentally, this hooter appears to be all but identical with that fitted by Stephens in about 1912 to *Gazelle*, which she still carries. The railmotor also seems to have a single acetylene lamp in mid cabin with some sort of associated container on the front of the guard's end. The new boiler was also almost certainly the cause of a piece of work that Rolvenden probably carried out and should have been, and probably was, ashamed of. Two ugly doors were inserted in the driver's end next to the boiler, with strap hinges of such crudity that later commentators, with some justice, compared them to garden shed doors. However practical this might have been, its appearance was the cause of some unjustified ridicule of the whole railmotor concept. The boiler also required a new feed pipe to be somewhat crudely plumbed in from the water tank. On a brighter note, she probably also changed her identity at this time from her original designation of coach No 16 to the more dignified locomotive No 6. This increase in status seems to have been achieved simply by repainting the middle body panels from ivory to brown and adding 'K&ESR No. 6' in screw-on iron lettering. This gave a less flamboyant but no doubt more practical finish. Interestingly, the internal vestibule was not repainted but kept its middle panel painted ivory until the end.

Mechanically, the railmotor might have settled down to service, but conventional wisdom, supported by the lack of photographic or written evidence, suggests she never entered revenue-earning service. However, our first photograph of the railmotor, with its second boiler, taken in the 1908-1911 period, shows it displaying a Robertsbridge Junction destination board. Routine repairs such as re-tubing, commensurate with regular use, are given in the

Renumbered in the locomotive stock list as No. 6, this photograph, taken between 1908 and 1911, shows that the waist panel has been repainted brown to match the lower half of the side. Note the destination board (inset) reading 'Robertsbridge Jn'. Does this suggest that it had been in passenger service? *CSRM*

**A later photograph showing the incongruous 'garden shed' doors and crude hinges, all by then in a damaged state.** *CSRM*

rolling stock register for the years 1909, 1910, 1911 and 1913. The public timetables for the period 1908-14, moreover, do show potential diagrams around sundry Tenterden-Robertsbridge Junction short workings. K&ESR's weekday public timetable for the summer of 1909 confirms that it was scheduled to run as follows under the note M: Motor Car, one class only:

|  | a.m. | a.m. | p.m. | p.m. | p.m. | W & SO p.m. |
|---|---|---|---|---|---|---|
| Dep. Robertsbridge Junction: | 7.50 | 11.25 | 12.40 | 4.25 | 8*i*37 | 9.33 |
| Dep. Bodiam (for Staplecross): | 8.02 | 11.37 | 12.59 | 4.36 | 8*i*47 | 9.43 |
| Dep. Northiam (for Beckley & Sandhurst): | 8.14 | 11.50 | 1.6 | 4.50 | 8*i*57 | 9.53 |
| Dep. Wittersham Road: | 8.22 | – | 1.15 | 4.59 | 9*i* 7 | 10. 0 |
| Dep. Rolvenden: | 8.42 | – | 1.26 | 5.7 | 9*i*17 | 10. 8 |
| Arr. Tenterden Town: | 8.50 | – | – | – | – | 10.16 |

|  | a.m. | a.m. | p.m. | SO p.m. | SX p.m. |
|---|---|---|---|---|---|
| Dep. Tenterden Town: | - | - | - | - | - |
| Dep. Rolvenden: | 6.45 | 9.30 | - | 2.30 | 3.20 |
| Dep. Wittersham Road: | 6.54 | 9.40 | - | 2.41 | 3.31 |
| Dep. Northiam (for Beckley & Sandhurst): | 7. 4 | 9.53 | 12.0 | 3.19 | 3.43 |
| Dep. Bodiam (for Staplecross): | 7.17 | 10. 5 | 12.13 | 3.32 | 3.57 |
| arr. Robertsbridge Junction: | 7.30 | 10.20 | 12.26 | 3.45 | 4.10 |

*i*: Except Wednesdays and Saturdays. SO: Sats. Only. SX: Sats. Excepted. W: Weds. only.

Further, *Bradshaw's Guide* in August/September 1909 and September 1913 shows specific services footnoted for a Motor Car and the footnote continued into mid-1914. There is no doubt, therefore, that she did enter regular service, albeit somewhat intermittently. Perhaps she was, in the event, at least as successful, both mechanically and as a traffic machine, as the contemporary railcars of the larger railways. Unfortunately, we know of no photographs of the railmotor in service, nor of any contemporary accounts of its service on the line. It must have been in use to have justified the repairs carried out and when an additional siding was put in at Bodiam in 1910, Stephens requested permission to erect a small platform alongside it so that the railcar could use it to pass.

Substantial body repairs were evidently called for and probably carried out in June 1913. These involved the replacement of cracked side panels near the boiler, and replacement and alteration of the beading on the guard's end panels. At this overhaul, too, she probably lost her smart ivory and brown livery to adopt the then standard overall brown. The guard's end was substantially altered shortly after this time, with the old three-window layout replaced by a more practical two-window arrangement.

Despite all this work, the experiment was reaching its conclusion. The railmotor seems to have come to the end of its operational life sometime around 1914, following failure in service at Wittersham Road. It was certainly recorded as non-operational in 1915. The widow of Nelson Wood, a long-time K&ESR employee and petrol railmotor driver, reported to researchers in the 1970s that her end had come directly as a result of failure to generate sufficient steam to surmount that enemy of all under-powered trains, Tenterden bank. One wonders how many times this had occurred before, and why this event should have finally brought its service to an end.

No 6 did not 'go gently into that good night'. The subsequent history of the railmotor is one of gradual decay in the yard at Rolvenden. Nevertheless, she was clearly a favourite child of Stephens and she was kept in good repair throughout the Great War period of government control. She had become sufficiently well known in technical circles for Kyrle Willans, one of the principal originators of the use of Sentinel engine units into locomotives and railcars, to refer favourably to her conception, and she survived in good order well into the era of these, her moral successors and cousins. The heyday of these successful machines in the mid-1920s saw the Pickering carefully stored in Rolvenden

After the alterations carried out in 1913, the railmotor was repainted in the then standard overall brown. The original of this photograph was presented in c.1926 by Colonel Stephens to A. B. MacLeod, the Southern Railway's Superintendent on the Isle of Wight.  *CSRM*

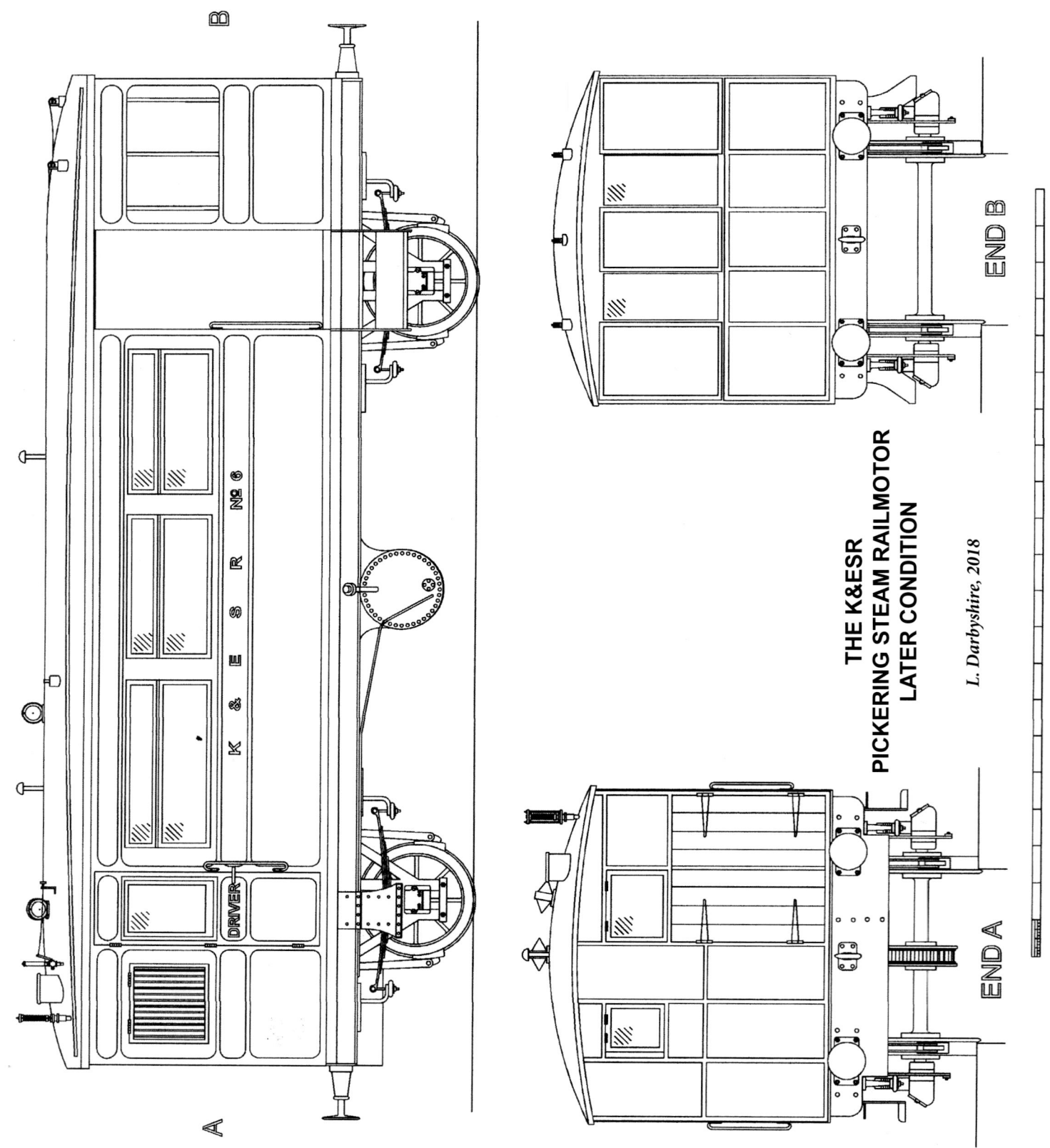

An informal shot, taken in the 1930s, showing that the internal vestibule had not been repainted, but kept its ivory middle panel until the end. *CSRM*

sidings and, when her panelling deteriorated, she was extensively repaired. Her old single long side-panel on her most photographed left side was replaced with two new ones, complete with matching beading, and two other panels here were replaced. Did the Colonel have plans to replace the Achilles heel of old-fashioned and worn steam plant with internal combustion engines, or more up-to-date steam units such as the Sentinel, which, by then, was reliable, relatively cheap and probably available second-hand off steam lorries? We know that a couple of the latest Sentinel locomotives were tested on the Shropshire & Montgomeryshire in 1927. Did this raise, ever for a while, his interest sufficiently to get repairs done with the available scarce funds? Did the availability of the K&ESR's third petrol railcar, bought in 1929, finally kill off any interest? We do not know.

With Stephens' death, all hope dissipated and, in 1932, his successor, the essentially practical W. H. Austen, applied to the Court of Chancery for permission to dispose of a number of surplus and worn-out items of rolling stock. These included the railmotor, saying: The steam rail car... has not been used for at least 15 years and is quite beyond repair. Its scrap value I estimate at the sum of £6/10/-. Even at this price, no buyer seems to have been forthcoming and the railmotor visibly disintegrated at various Rolvenden locations over the next ten years. It appears to have remained substantially complete until 1935 when the double doors to the engine compartment disappeared and portions of the panelling and roof canvas began to lift. Some time after 1937, much of its plumbing appears to have been removed and almost the entire panel above the windows on the left side had come adrift. The body of the railmotor was reported as broken up and burnt in late 1939 and the frame in 1941, though K&ESR records state that her remains were sold for scrap to Messrs Cohen's on the 25th May 1944. Perhaps this was simply the last remains of all as, according to Austen's son, its frame provided the materials for the construction of a new water tower at Rolvenden in the Autumn of 1943. The water tower escaped the general destruction of the Rolvenden site by British Railways and is still in use today.

The railmotor deteriorating in Rolvenden yard, September 1935. *CSRM*

Deteriorating a little further, 21st September 1935. *H. C. Casserley*

The underframe of ex-L&SWR 'Ilfracombe Goods' 0-6-0 *Rother* sits in front of the Pickering steam railmotor in the yard at Rolvenden which attracted so many enthusiasts, because of the ancient relics. 21st May 1939. *J. Baker*

The railmotor in terminal decline. The 'garden shed' doors have dropped off, revealing the second larger boiler in its offset position c.1937.
*Jim Pedor/IRS*

A view from the other end, showing the arrangement of the windows, but with one wheel set missing, 29th July 1939.
*S. W. Baker*

The new water tower at Rolvenden constructed by W. H. Austen in the autumn of 1943. It is said to incorporate parts from the Pickering steam railmotor. The tower is used regularly by the K&ESR heritage railway. The Terrier and the Class 'O1' pictured were regular performers on the line before closure. *CSFM*

The first, small, WC&PR Drewry petrol railmotor (No. 1) as delivered, probably in Drewry's standard livery of dark green with the company's title in a garter. Note the three large windows along the side which could be dropped to their full depth, providing plenty of fresh air in hot weather. *Drewry Official*

# – CHAPTER 3 –

# THE WESTON, CLEVEDON & PORTISHEAD RAILWAY'S DREWRY RAILMOTORS

Holman Stephens showed an early interest in internal combustion engines and demonstrated this by continually, and accurately, referring to what we now call 'Diesels' as 'Ackroyd-Stuarts', the true pioneer of such engines. There was a report in the 1920s that, in 1890, Stephens had motorised a tramcar bogie. However, Rodney Weaver, a notable historian of such matters, carefully researched this area. The world's first such locomotive was built, with a French-designed petrol engine, in the USA. In 1893, one was shipped to London and ran experimentally in Greenwich and Croydon for much of the year and was inspected by the Tramways Institute in July of that year. Weaver speculated that Stephens had seen that locomotive during the short period of its trials, which may have triggered his interest in replicating it with an Ackroyd-Stuart engine. However it was unlikely that Stephens was actively involved in such important early trials.

Stephens, in undertaking his first independent assignment, the Rye and Camber Tramway, proposed in March 1895 the use of an oil motor on a passenger bogie car. After the Connelly motor trial, the first known English locomotive was built in Hull in 1894 and the first fully successful locomotive was not built until July 1896 for the narrow gauge Woolwich Arsenal system. Such engines were, at this stage, extremely bulky, low-powered and temperamental. Weaver again speculated whether this might have actually been built, but once more found no evidence. Wiser counsels prevailed and, although originally specifying it was a temporary measure whilst the oil motor was being constructed (or it did not work well), Stephens reverted to steam for the Rye and Camber. For the next few years he used good steam modern designs, when they could be afforded.

Following the First World War, and the technical progress engendered by it, Stephens turned his mind back to the internal combustion engine owing to the increased cost of working and to avoid curtailing the number of trains.

Much attention is given in the Stephens' cannon to the back-to-back railmotors derived from Ford and Shefflex road vehicles. However, his first effort at a petrol railmotor came from a very different, railway-based tradition that was developed by the Drewry Company. This was very successful and eventually led to the purchase of a second-hand railmotor from the same source. Neither of these railmotors attracted the interest of the later motors, perhaps because Stephens did not make wider use of such cars, probably on the grounds of initial (and spares) costs, and their success has consequently been unfairly overlooked.

## The Small Drewry

The Drewry Company (it had various legal titles over the years) was a pioneer design and sales company for lightweight railway vehicles, which used a variety of other companies, principally the Baguley companies over the years to construct its designs. Drewry was particularly successful in selling lightweight and fairly reliable petrol trolleys from the Edwardian period, and they produced a standard range. By the end of the First World War, they had moved into producing larger machines of greater than 20hp using Baguley (another company that had various legal titles over the years) engineering and expertise. Stephens was an early customer, having somehow inveigled the necessary money from the receivers of the Weston, Clevedon and Portishead, ordering a railmotor on the 15th February 1921.

This new vehicle, nominally a Drewry, was constructed by Baguley Cars Ltd and it carried their works number 1252. Recorded by some sources as delivered in October 1921, work records show it as April 1922. This disparity may be explained by a peculiarity of the order that the car had to be approved on its completion by the Engineer of the Royal Automobile Club or his deputy - a condition certainly imposed by Stephens using friends at his usual London luncheon venue to cover his lack of direct internal combustion expertise. It may well have been wise and fruitful, for works records show that the railmotor was modified to comply with regulations for petrol cars in public service.

The railmotor was largely based on standard mechanical parts used by the builder, with a water-cooled Baguley engine that had four cylinders, each with a bore of 4in. and stroke of 5in. It was capable of developing 25hp, having a three-speed gearbox with the final drive by inverted tooth chain to one of the axles giving a maximum speed about 25mph on the level. Reverse gear gave all three speeds and there were controls at each end, although the brake and gear

**In this view of the small Drewry at the Weston terminus, the elaborate garter has given way to simple lettering, possibly in yellow.** *CSRM*

levers had to be removed from the cups into which they fitted. The four wheels were 2ft in diameter and were of chilled iron, as opposed to the normal steel, by British Griffin, and the wheelbase was a little longer than customary at 9ft, with the normal Drewry inside suspension. It weighed six tons. Originally, the petrol tank was inside the car body, but, for safety reasons, it was later replaced by a horizontal cylinder above one buffer-beam. The exhaust pipe rose to above roof level and there was a whistle hinged to it and held at an angle by means of a spring. This was operated by pulling a wire inside the car, which effectively joined the whistle to the end of the exhaust pipe, a device Stephens returned to on later railmotors. Petrol consumption was stated by the makers to be 16 mpg on easy grades, which worked out at a running cost of about 6d per train mile.

The enclosed body was 19ft long and 8ft wide, seating thirty Third Class on wooden-slatted seats with a central gangway, with room for another twelve standing. It was of three-ply wood panelling covered with thin steel sheeting. There were three large windows on either side, which could be dropped to their full depth for ample ventilation, plus three large windows on each end. Lighting was by acetylene, but electric lights seem to have been provided by 1927. Doors were on either side at each end, with steps to give access from track level. The roof, which was only 8ft 3in. from rail level (making it much lower than a normal railway carriage) was railed around so that luggage could be carried on it, a virtually unused feature it shared with Stephens' later railmotors; access was by a ladder at each end. Radiators were located beneath the substantial buffer beams at each end, with side buffers at normal height, which emphasised the low roof. Originally fitted with three-link couplings, these were replaced with screw couplings to cope with its later trailers. A lamp bracket was located to the right of the coupling at one end and to the left at the other.

The railmotor was probably painted in the standard Drewry livery of dark green with yellow lining and, on delivery, it had the company's title in a smart garter on the sides. In the 1930s this was replaced by the initials 'WC & PR'.

Inadequate seating for other than the quietest days was soon apparent. To give the railmotor more versatility, trailers were developed. A photograph shows the small Drewry coupled to the former Metropolitan Railway four-wheeled coach, No. 7, which the WC&P used as a spare for its usual fixed sets. It is highly unlikely that it was used in public

WC&PR Small Drewry and the ex Metropolitan Railway carriage (WC&P No. 7) at Clevedon in 1921. The coach survives in preservation at the London Transport Museum as MET No. 353.
*Howard Carey collection*

service with the Drewry, which was too light to have braked the heavier coach (c10 tons). The railmotor did not have continuous brakes, a feature it shared with later cars – all in clear breach of statutory requirements.

A purpose-built trailer was ordered from Drewry in November 1922 and delivered in March 1923. Described by its builders as enclosed, it was, in fact, of a semi-open type without windows and, so curtains provided the only protection against the weather. It seated twenty-four, a figure often exceeded at busy times. Side windows were ultimately added sometime after 1929. Like the railmotor, the trailer was painted green with yellow lettering, but by closure of the line it was in plain dark-green. After withdrawal, the body is reported to have become a summerhouse in a garden at Chiseldon, near Swindon.

Later, it became apparent that the addition of a goods trailer would enable the railmotor to handle the extensive milk churn traffic and a small wagon, No. 19, an ex MR three-plank drop-side wagon, was adapted for use with the railmotor. However, like the earlier coach, the wagon proved too heavy for the limited haulage and braking power available, and a special one was ordered from Cranes of Dereham to run with the railmotor instead. This was delivered on the 21st September, 1925. It had a capacity of 3 tons 10cwt. and it was fitted with a three-plank body measuring 12ft x

The trailer for the small Drewry pictured before delivery to the WC&PR. Described by the builders as enclosed, it was, as can be seen, open to the elements. Curtains were soon fitted.
*CSRM*

After 1929 full sides with new doors were fitted to the trailer at Clevedon, the end seats were full benches and the brakes completely removed!
*CSRM*

The wagon, built by Cranes of Dereham, can be seen behind the small Drewry, loaded with milk churns. It was needed for the extensive milk traffic, replacing an ex-MR wagon which had proved to be too heavy.
*CSRM*

The small Drewry standing with its trailer at Clevedon in the 1930s, which has acquired its windows and could now accurately be described as enclosed, but the railmotor has lost its number. *CSRM*

7ft, with sides 18in. high. Screw couplings and side-buffers of normal height were fitted.

The railmotor, with its trailers, was so successful that by 1927 its mileage exceeded that of all the steam locomotives put together. The summer timetable only required the railmotor and one steam engine, the latter being used on the trains that ran through to Portishead and were, therefore, normally mixed because of the quarry traffic at that end of the line. For the same reason, it was necessary to use one steam engine working services, with one passenger coach, in winter.

The small Drewry and trailer, quite well loaded, crossing the road near Walton Park in the 1920s. Note how exposed the railmotor is as it crosses the road at an angle. *CSRM*

Small Drewry and trailer, both well-loaded, awaiting departure at the Weston terminus, in the mid-1920s.   *CSRM*

A busy moment at Clevedon on Easter bank holiday, the 9th April 1928. The small Drewry and its trailer are crowded, illustrating that inter-connection of trains was a complicated business at the single platform at Clevedon. It also shows that railmotors were unsuitable for heavy traffic. The Terrier, No. 2 *Portishead* was acquired by the WC&PR after the Drewry and its trailer.   *CSRM (Peter Strange Collection/H. G. W. Household)*

Another good load of passengers fill the small Drewry, seen here leaving Clevedon station. *CSRM (Peter Strange Collection)*

The views were not quite as panoramic in the large Drewry railmotor as they were on this, the first small one. *CSRM*

The small Drewry and a full load of passengers waits to leave Weston terminus. Note the mixture of conventional sleepers and concrete 'pots' in the trackwork. The pots were an innovation by Stephens to aid maintenance.
*CSRM (Peter Strange Collection)*

Small Drewry on a fine day with the windows fully open entering Portishead station in the late 1930s. Note the petrol tank fixed to the front of the railmotor. Mustad's nail factory and siding are on the left of the Drewry.
*CSRM (Peter Strange Collection)*

The small Drewry has come to grief in an accident with a brewer's van on the Bristol Road level crossing, much to the amusement of the schoolchildren.
*CSRM (Peter Strange Collection)*

**H. G. W. Household captured this moment on the 13th July 1927, following an accident to a brake van empty milk churns from it are being placed in the trailer, closely observed by schoolboys.** *CSRM (Peter Strange Collection/H. G. W. Household)*

**One of the many level crossing gates on the line being opened for the small Drewry.** *CSRM*

Two views of the small Drewry in the yard at Clevedon. *both CSRM*

What later became known as the WC&PR large Drewry in fully-lined out Southern Railway livery. It appears to be on a demonstration run judging by the formal dress of the passengers. *CSRM*

## The Large Drewry

**M**eanwhile, elsewhere, the Southern Railway was seeking economical solutions to providing services on some of its minor branch lines. As a result, in April 1927, the General Manager instigated a review of operating these services by steam or petrol-engine railmotors. To test the latter, a Drewry railmotor was ordered, but there is considerable variation in reported dates of the order and delivery. The Drewry Board minutes record that it had been ordered in March 1927, but Bradley, in his largely definitive *Locomotives of the Southern Railway, Part 1*, RCTS, 1975, which was probably based on now lost Southern records, gives June 1927. Whatever the original order date, R. E. L. Maunsell took a personal interest in the deliberations and specifications, even over quite minor matters, which seem to have changed over the months. It took until August 1927 for the Southern to harden its requirement to a four-wheeled car with full railway buffing and drawgear to seat 26, and to include a guard's compartment to carry milk churns. It is interesting to speculate whether Stephens, who was friendly with both Maunsell and his General Manager, was informally consulted for his experience during these deliberations.

The order was finally placed on the 13th December, 1927 for what the Southern designated a branch line car. Its passengers sat on moquette-upholstered seats with reversible backs and entered the passenger compartment by a doorway slightly over halfway along the body. Beyond this was a luggage compartment for twenty-eight milk churns, equipped with double doors and accessible by a sliding door from the passenger area. When delivered, internal illumination was provided by electric lighting. The doors to the passenger compartment were fitted with steps three treads deep, whilst the driver's doors and luggage compartment doors only had double tread steps. With a body length of 31ft and a wheelbase of 20ft, the body was far nearer normal railway practice than the earlier car, for Drewry had by then adopted a more conventional approach of suspension and radiator type and the body reflected this. The driver had his own cab at each end which, at the powered end, had its own side doors; the further driving cab could only be entered from the luggage compartment.

The views were not quite as panoramic as they were from the first WC&P railmotor, as passengers had no forward or backward view, although the five-side windows with inwardly hinged toplights

**Passengers sat on red and black moquette-upholstered seats with reversible backs and entered the passenger compartment by a doorway slightly over halfway along the body.** *CSRM*

**A luggage compartment for twenty-eight milk churns was equipped with double doors and was accessible by a sliding door from the passenger area.** *CSRM*

provided a good outlook. Roof ventilators were also fitted, and the windows in the passenger doors could be dropped to their full depth for additional fresh air on hot days. The driver's compartments were fitted with two forward windows separated by a large central panel and by side windows that could be dropped to full depth. The right-hand window at each end was fitted with a windscreen wiper mounted at the base, and the Southern subsequently fitted a single headlight below the roofline at the centre of each end, a direct reflection of the alteration made in 1927 to the WC&P motor. Three lamp brackets were fitted along the top edge of the buffer beam. At the powered end, a coupling hook seems to have been provided, but the other end was fitted with a three-link coupling. Screw couplings do not ever seem to have been fitted to this railmotor.

The body proved rather large for its 50hp engine, which gave a great deal of trouble in service, particularly due to vibration. Transmission was through a three-speed gearbox operated in both forward and reverse. Delivered on the 21st May, 1928, the Southern railmotor had a seating capacity of 26 and it weighed 10 tons 17cwt.

Even after all the design deliberations, it failed to please. Bradley reports that at first there were major issues with the gearbox, but the problems actually centred on the engine, which was of an outdated and inadequate Baguley design.

Reportedly, the Andover to Romsey services were taken over and worked quite satisfactorily until the extra traffic created overwhelmed the railmotor's capacity. By July 1928, it was reported working between Reading and Blackwater and, in April 1929, the Appledore - New Romney - Dungeness services. However, during 1929, serious engine problems were encountered – Drewry staff recalled that they were authorised to offer a new engine of Baguley build, but records show the original engine was modified and reconditioned at Andover in 1929. This clearly indicates that the railmotor was still on the Romsey service at that date. When the WC&P inspected it with a view to purchase, it was working the Fareham to Gosport line.

Because of these problems, the Southern did not immediately take the railmotor into stock, or pay the £1,850 due for it. Difficulties with the Baguley engines seem to have been a major factor in precipitating a split between the Drewry and Baguley companies, which occurred in March 1930, after six months notice had been given. Bradley records that a major breakdown occurred in February 1930. Drewry, worried about its reputation with the poor performance of a car so much in the public eye, fitted a Parsons M4 engine that developed 64hp from 5in. x 6in. cylinders, which it was claimed cured all the troubles. Bradley also reported that seating was reduced at this time, but this does not seem to have actually occurred, and capacity was, later on, still 26. The Southern did not take final delivery from Drewry, or pay their bill, until mid-1933.

Having now paid for the railmotor and, having a reputedly reliable unit, the Southern now clearly lost interest in this machine. No doubt, W. H. Austen, through his Southern contacts, had noted this, with the result that in July 1934 it was seen at Bristol en route for service on the WC&P, at £272 a bargain for him and a big loss to the Southern. The railmotor then seems to have settled into a quiet revenue-earning existence, quite different from its development period on the Southern.

As was customary for Austen, little effort was made to alter the railmotor's appearance and its Southern livery was largely retained, including its number 5. The words 'SOUTHERN RAILWAY' were painted out and 'W.C.& P.' painted on. It kept this livery until the final winter of the line when all lining disappeared. The larger railmotor's seating accommodation was less than that of the original Drewry, but it took on that vehicle's duties to a large extent and it was not uncommon to see the passenger trailer car attached to No. 5.

When traffic ceased in 1940, the Great Western Railway purchased the Weston, Clevedon & Portishead's rolling stock. The larger railmotor was marshalled in a train of WC&P carriages and travelled to Swindon on its own wheels, but the original railmotor and its trailer possibly travelled there on well wagons. The body of the larger railmotor was purchased by a Swindon girls' school for use as a pavilion, but the other vehicles were probably broken up for scrap.

**The large Drewry at Clevedon in October 1937 with its new identity as WC&PR No. 5, but otherwise retaining the full SR Maunsell passenger livery.** *CSRM/R. G. Jarvis*

The large Drewry taken from the milk churn platform at Mud Lane bound for Weston. Driver Morgan and guard Jack Riddick can be seen in driver's compartment. *CSRM (Peter Strange Collection)*

There's not much sign of the Maunsell lining now, but that may be due to the film in use at that time.  *CSRM*

A well-loaded train consisting of the large Drewry and trailer awaiting departure at Weston.  *CSRM*

**Passing Wick St. Lawrence the large Drewry and the trailer are heading for Weston in June 1937.**
*CSRM (Peter Strange Collection)*

**The large Drewry and trailer on Yeo bridge, near Wick St. Lawrence heading for Clevedon in June 1937.**
*CSRM (Peter Strange Collection)*

**Bound for Portishead the large Drewry is seen crossing the road at Clevedon All Saints in September 1936. The crossing gates are reflected in the cab windows.**
*CSRM (Peter Strange Collection)*

**A final view of the large Drewry.**
*CSRM (Peter Strange Collection)*

The Shropshire & Montgomeryshire Railway three-car set complete with a baggage truck. This damaged photograph has fortunately survived. A note on the back records that it was given by Stephens in 1926 to A. B. McLeod, the Southern Railway's Superintendent on the Isle of Wight. *CSRM*

# – CHAPTER 4 –

# THE FORD RAILMOTORS AND THEIR DIRECT ANCESTOR

### The Wolseley-Siddeley

The Weston Clevedon & Portishead Railway had received a modern and efficient vehicle courtesy of a well-funded Receiver, but it was effectively a hand-built one-off product and, therefore, too expensive to adopt on most cash-starved independent light railways. With this in mind, sometime before 1921, Stephens had begun experimenting on the Kent and East Sussex Railway with a cheaper alternative for trial as a rail lorry and then as a bus. He had a Wolseley-Siddeley motor car, fitted with pressed-steel-disc flanged wheels of the type made by Lynton Wheel & Tyre Co., Longford Bridge, Warrington, for use on cars and light lorries.

This was not an entirely new idea, because the Caledonian Railway had converted a motor charabanc to operate its somewhat obscure Connel Ferry Bridge shuttle service in 1911. However, in using such adaptations Stephens was at the forefront of world practice, for only a few lines in North America and one French manufacturer were trying such things at the time, and the North Eastern Railway's adaptation of a 1921 Leyland bus did not go into service until July 1922.

The motor car was of some vintage, for the Wolseley-Siddeley brand of Wolseley Motors Ltd had only existed from 1905 to 1911, and it had a chain drive of a type that had only been in use from 1906 to 1909. On the 9th June 1917, Stephens had advertised in the *Army and Navy Gazette*:

**MOTOR WAGONETTE**, Sidersley-Wolseley [sic], 18 22. h.p. (open), to carry 12 persons, for SALE. Converts into 15 cwt. lorry in 5 minutes, for luggage purposes. Complete, £100. Will sell for £75 after crisis. Apply, Col. H. F. STEPHENS, Tonbridge, Kent.

This followed on from an advert in the *Eastbourne Gazette* a month earlier for an apparently similar vehicle. If unsold this may well be the vehicle converted for rail use. The first evidence of the existence of the rail conversion vehicle emerged in an undated photograph found at Messrs Drake & Fletcher, motor engineers of Maidstone, Kent, but unfortunately the company has no record of it. Nor do the K&ESR records shed any light on the subject, but it was more than likely the staff at Rolvenden

Undated photograph found at Messrs Drake & Fletcher, motor engineers of Maidstone of the Wolseley-Siddeley motor car chassis at Rolvenden with rail wheels and lettered K&ESR. Unfortunately, the company has no record of this vehicle, nor is there anything in the K&ESR records

CSRM

Official photograph of the Wolseley-Siddeley railmotor taken at Rolvenden, showing the chain drive to the rear axle. According to Arthur Iggulden, a long-term Stephens employee, the body was built 'in a cow shed in Vale Road, Tonbridge', very close to 23, Salford Terrace, the headquarters of the Stephens empire. *CSRM*

were aware of it. The photograph shows a chassis with a square, flat platform for carrying light goods, with the lettering K&ESR painted on the side. The driver sat on a bench seat, the width of the chassis, completely open to the elements and importantly, like the WC&PR's petrol railmotor, an additional radiator had been hung from the chassis at the rear to facilitate reverse running.

According to K&ESR employee C. R. Blair, the vehicle saw little use, but it must have been moderately successful in this guise, because fairly soon a passenger body was built for it, according to Arthur Iggulden, a long-term Stephens employee, 'in a cow shed in Vale Road, Tonbridge', Kent. Very basic, with no mudguards, headlights or buffing gear, it probably had seats for fourteen or so passengers. It would most likely have undergone some trials on the K&ESR, but the railmotor was then transferred to the Colonel's Selsey Tramway to enter service there on the 11th March 1924. To begin with, it must have operated by itself, with the driver looking over his shoulder whilst travelling in reverse, until about a month later, when an adapted Ford lorry arrived on the Tramway, with which it worked back-to-back as a form of 'mixed' train. The Wolseley-Siddeley was not liked by staff at Selsey. Herbert Warwick, who drove on the Tramway from 1923 to 1926, recollected that it was extremely difficult to start and that the rear radiator was smashed when the railmotor was being turned on the Southern turntable at Chichester. It was transferred to the Shropshire & Montgomeryshire Light Railway, probably in the autumn of 1927, and it seems to have been repainted into S&MR blue livery. Many think that it did not work there, but railcar mileages recorded over the period 1927-29 were higher than would have been possible with the one resident set, so perhaps it did turn a wheel in revenue-earning service in Shropshire.

For nine years it mouldered away on the rear siding at Kinnerley, but in 1936 it received a new lease of life when, with the chassis and engine, etc., discarded and cut up, the body of the railmotor was transferred to the ex-LCC horse tram chassis and it re-emerged with *Gazelle* in June 1937, in a matching olive-green livery to form an inspection train. Access to the saloon, like its predecessor, was from between the four-foot, the rear-hinged outward opening doors on either side towards the front of the vehicle, were sealed up and a similar centrally mounted sliding door to that in the rear bulkhead was added at the

*Above*: The Wolseley-Siddeley being delivered on a well wagon to the Selsey Tramway at Chichester. Note the absence of any decorative features and any draw gear. *CSRM*

*Left*: The Ford rail lorry shown at Selsey shed back-to-back with the Wolseley-Siddeley. The pair could run in the classic Stephens railmotor manner. In one direction the lorry would pull the Wolseley-Siddeley and in the other direction the lorry would trail. Importantly the driver could be at the front of the leading vehicle. *CSRM*

front. One of the vertical brake wheels from the original vehicle was added to the nearside front of the body to continue its original purpose of working the brakes via chains. The toplights of the four windows on each side opened inwards from the bottom to provide ventilation.

*Gazelle* and her trailer were also available for private hire. On several occasions they were hired by groups of railway enthusiasts for trips over the line before the outbreak of war. The trailer continued in use as a light coach with *Gazelle* until sometime during the Second World War, probably in late 1942, when it was reported that the chassis broke its back.

It was still not the end for this pioneering vehicle's body, for it became a grounded hut and, by the 1950s, it could seen be alongside the Criggion branch line as a lineman's shed about a quarter of a mile from Kinnerley. It was surveyed and measured by members of the Colonel Stephens Railway Museum in 1975,

*Gazelle* and the trailer with Wolseley-Siddeley body departing Kinnerley Junction for Llanymynech. *CSRM*

when it was found to be approximately 13ft 9in. long by 7ft 6in. wide and 5ft 8in. high. The frame was pitch pine, with tongue-and-groove floorboards on top, and the main body uprights were 2in. square ash. Windows were plate glass and metal strips reinforced the uprights. The arched roof was covered with tongue-and-groove boards and heavy-duty hessian-backed canvas, then covered in pitch. The wooden body frame was, by then, clad externally in steel and lined with wooden planks internally below the waist, but no trace remained of any internal fittings or original paintwork. They regrettably concluded that what was left of the body was beyond repair and would soon disintegrate, so that it could not be rescued.

However, in 1986, the body was rediscovered by Mike Wright of Myddle, near Shrewsbury, and it was carefully dismantled and removed for safe-keeping to his garden. With a little work having been carried out, ten years later, on the 9th September 1996, the body was removed to the 2ft 6in. gauge Ystwyth Valley Railway at Trawscoed, near Aberystwyth, Cardiganshire, where it was hoped it would be fully restored. It was kept under a tarpaulin, but no work was carried out. The tarpaulin began to disintegrate over time, causing further deterioration of the body. Alas, in about 2006, vandals broke into the site and made a bonfire of the Wolseley remains, together with a coach body and other woodwork on the site, resulting in virtually total destruction. Previously, Jon Clarke, an enthusiast interested in the S&MR had rescued the very last piece of the railmotor at Kinnerley, a displaced 2ft-long section of a sidewall spur from below the windows. This resides on display today as a kind of holy relic in the museum at Tenterden.

**For many years the remains of the Wolseley-Siddeley could be seen alongside the Criggion Branch of the S&MR in use as a lineman's shed about a quarter of a mile from Kinnerley and remained in situ even after the closure of the line.**
*David Churchill Collection & CSRM*

# THE FORD RAILMOTORS

An official photograph of the first K&ESR Ford set, as delivered, at Tenterden.  *CSRM*

## The Ford Railmotors

Perhaps encouraged by his work with the elderly Wolseley-Siddeley chassis, Stephens bought some cheap mass-produced Ford Motor Company's 1-ton lorry chassis (part of the Model T family) with bus bodies on them, using the same pressed-steel wheels. To avoid the reversing problem, he used them in back-to-back pairs. This was a little wasteful in that the leading car had to pull the trailing car, which was an unnecessary deadweight, but it obviated the need to have a full reverse gearbox, or to turn the vehicle.

## The Kent and East Sussex Railway Set No. 1

The first set was delivered to the K&ESR sometime in late 1922, being described and illustrated in the *Commercial Motor* magazine of the 12th December that year:

### PETROL RAILCARS IN TANDEM
### A Novel Adaption of the Ordinary Ford Chassis

We have often had occasion in the past to refer to the adaption of ordinary road vehicles to rail uses, and those of our readers who are interested in this subject will undoubtedly give attention to the illustration which is published on this page, and which shows two Ford rail cars supplied by Messrs. Edmonds' Motors, of Thetford, Norfolk, to Colonel H. F. Stephens.

Ordinary Ford chassis are used for these rail cars, and should it be necessary they can be coupled and run back-to-back, for which purpose a centre buffer and draw-pin combined are employed. When it is desired to travel in the forward direction the gearing of the rear vehicle is placed in neutral. In the construction of these rail cars an independent gearbox is fitted, and, of course, the ordinary steering gear is dismantled and a solid axle fitted with flanged wheels similar to those which are used at the rear. When operating in this manner no difficulty has been experienced in maintaining a good average speed.

There is a sliding door fitted at the back of each vehicle, so that when the two cars are coupled no difficulty is experienced in gaining access to the interior of the one body from the other.

Later, in September 1923, Stephens wrote to the same magazine, saying: '*I have nine small steam railways under my control and am trying several forms of motor trains.... In a previous experiment I learnt, to my sorrow, that it is cheaper to have a car at each end than to put in a reverse gear.*' Colonel Stephens gave his reason for choosing Ford chassis as follows:

Head-on view of the first K&ESR Ford set pictured at Rolvenden. *CSRM*

*'The motive units are the much despised 1-ton Fords; we chose this type, as we can always get spares without delay and for no other reason'.*

The units were built on the lorry chassis, with the standard bonnet and mudguards retained, complete with sidelights, although these soon disappeared. Two headlamps were initially fitted and it is thought that one could be shaded red for reverse running. Again, these progressively disappeared, usually leaving only one operational, which, in the case of the K&ESR units, was moved to the centre of the roof. A lightweight wooden buffer bar was positioned above and in front of the headlamps, although the height and style of this fitting varied over the years. There were no couplings at the leading ends, until the second K&ESR set had its buffer bar lowered and couplings fitted to tow a trailer in the late 1920s. The units were connected by centre buffers with a single link-and-pin. The normal springing for contemporary road vehicles was retained, without shock absorbers, and with simple stops on the rear axle, resulting in often excessive roll. They were fitted with pressed-steel disc wheels, probably supplied by Lynton Wheel and Tyre Co., Longford Bridge, Warrington, and almost certainly virtually identical to their heavy-duty road wheels. These proved less than satisfactory, being noisy and liable to damage, and several different variants can be observed, possibly from other suppliers, such as Cranes (Dereham) Ltd. Pressed-steel 8-curved spoked wheels were tried on a later Selsey set, but eventually replacement disc wheels were settled on when necessary, probably of cast steel with three holes through the disc as on contemporary wagon wheels.

The bodies adhered to contemporary small rural bus standards, built from teak, reinforced by metal plates and with sheet metal covering below the waistline. Although supplied by Edmonds' Motors, the bodies of these, and subsequent Fords, were, in fact, constructed by Eaton Coachworks of Cringleford, Norfolk, this village now being virtually a suburb of Norwich. This was the trading name of the coachworks of H. E. Taylor & Co., a blacksmith and quality joiners business that had always made wagons, trolleys and tumbrels, and that, in the 1920s, successfully moved into buses and coaches, which became its major line of business until 1947. The railmotors were probably some of the earliest of such products.

Of five-bay construction, the large windows had an opening toplight, hinged at their bottom edge to open inwards, to provide ventilation (originally not on the rear bay of the first railmotor), below which the sides curved down in a neat tumblehome. The front window was divided into two equal sections with toplights, whilst the rear end was of similar design but with a sliding door in the centre. On either side of the driver, a front-hinged outward-opening door, with drop windows, gave access to the saloon, which had a gangway down the centre.

There were reversible seats for sixteen passengers. These were made up of narrow wooden slats with backrests consisting of nothing more than a 4-in. strip of wood attached to an iron frame, which was itself attached to the base of the seat. The livery was chocolate-brown and the roof, of shallow profile, domed and curved to the front, was painted white. The lighting is thought to have been originally by oil lamps. Soon after delivery, a full-length running board was added along the body on either side, but curved wheel arches above the rear wheels protruded untidily above it.

The petrol tank was originally under the driver's seat, but this had two disadvantages. First, the fumes leaked through the filler cap (this did not matter so much in the road lorries, which had open cabs, but it was unpleasant in the enclosed railmotor bodies). Second, it caused the seat to be mounted too high for some drivers, who could not reach the pedals.

The fuel tanks were subsequently moved outside and on the outside running boards, just to the rear of the driver's door; it was about 30 in. long, of an oval section, sitting on a curved base, held down by metal straps. It was boxed in, thus causing confusion amongst some commentators, who thought that it might be a tool box. The consequent lowering of the driver's seat caused the odd effect of the driver sitting far lower than his passengers. Certainly, later, according to Charles F. Klapper, writing in *The Railway Magazine* in September 1934, the seat was not attached to the floor so when the driver wished to apply the foot brake, he had to grip a handle fixed to the dashboard, otherwise his seat... would tip up.

The steering column remained in place (minus the steering wheel), upon which was mounted the hand-operated advance and retard spark lever on the left, and the hand throttle to the right. Foot controls were simple with three identical pedals, from left to right: low-neutral-high forward drive, reverse and transmission brake. The hand brake, when applied, stopped the left-hand pedal at neutral as well as operating the brake shoes on the front wheels. It was customary for the conductor/guard to travel in the rear unit where he could apply the hand brake in an emergency.

The gearbox was the normal 3-speed epicyclic Ford unit, which had a fixed ratio that was fine for light

**The first K&ESR Ford set showing the arrangement of the toplights at the front and side. Pictured at Tenterden, the headlights are in their original position. Note the flimsy buffer beam and the lack of draw gear.** *CSRM*

Taken from behind the driver, this photograph demonstrates both the poor visibility for the driver with central pillar immediately in front of him and his low seat position. There's not much comfort offered by the seats. *CSRM*

cars, but with heavier vans and buses proved to be a weakness. This was solved at an early date by the addition of a Supaphord Patented Auxiliary Gear Box supplied by a local Ford agent, Stanhay of Bank Street, Ashford, who in a letter of the 16th June 1923 referred to the supply of such a gearbox some time ago. These and other supplementary gearboxes manufactured by companies other than Ford, had come to the fore from 1922. Several designs were marketed, but Stephens chose the London-produced Supaphord, which gave an extra two forward and one reverse gear. There was a variety of standard ratios, and it is thought that the gear ratios were: Ford bottom gear 20 to 1, Supaphord Ford bottom gear 13.2 to 1, Ford top gear 7.2 to 1 and Supaphord Ford top gear 4.75 to 1. Also, importantly, the unit had a dog clutch, which enabled true freewheel when the rear unit was being towed, and might even have eased starting.

With their light design and single-axle drive, wheel spin was a problem, so a sand bucket was placed either side of the driver's seat, and an iron pipe, topped with a funnel, went through the floor to a shute in front of the rear wheels.

Warning systems consisted of an electric horn on the steering column and, latterly at least, a further and very unusual warning system. This was a tubular whistle, which was hinged to the end of the exhaust pipe, and normally held away from the pipe by a spring until operated by a driver-operated foot pedal, which pulled it over the exhaust outlet similar to that on the WC&PR's Drewry. A third device, a clearly visible klaxon, also appears to have been fitted to the S&MR set and may have been fitted to the others, but evidence is lacking.

The first Ford railmotor probably commenced normal service on Thursday, the 15th February 1923. Such was the novelty of these vehicles that Pathé News filmed the railmotor as it first entered service on the K&ESR. The film is still available.

Service details for the first few months of service, up to the 9th June, list, in passing, service failures (although unfortunately not specifying the reasons) and the trains on which they occurred. The railmotor appears to have been used during the trial period to directly replace steam services. They worked the 7.06am train from Tenterden

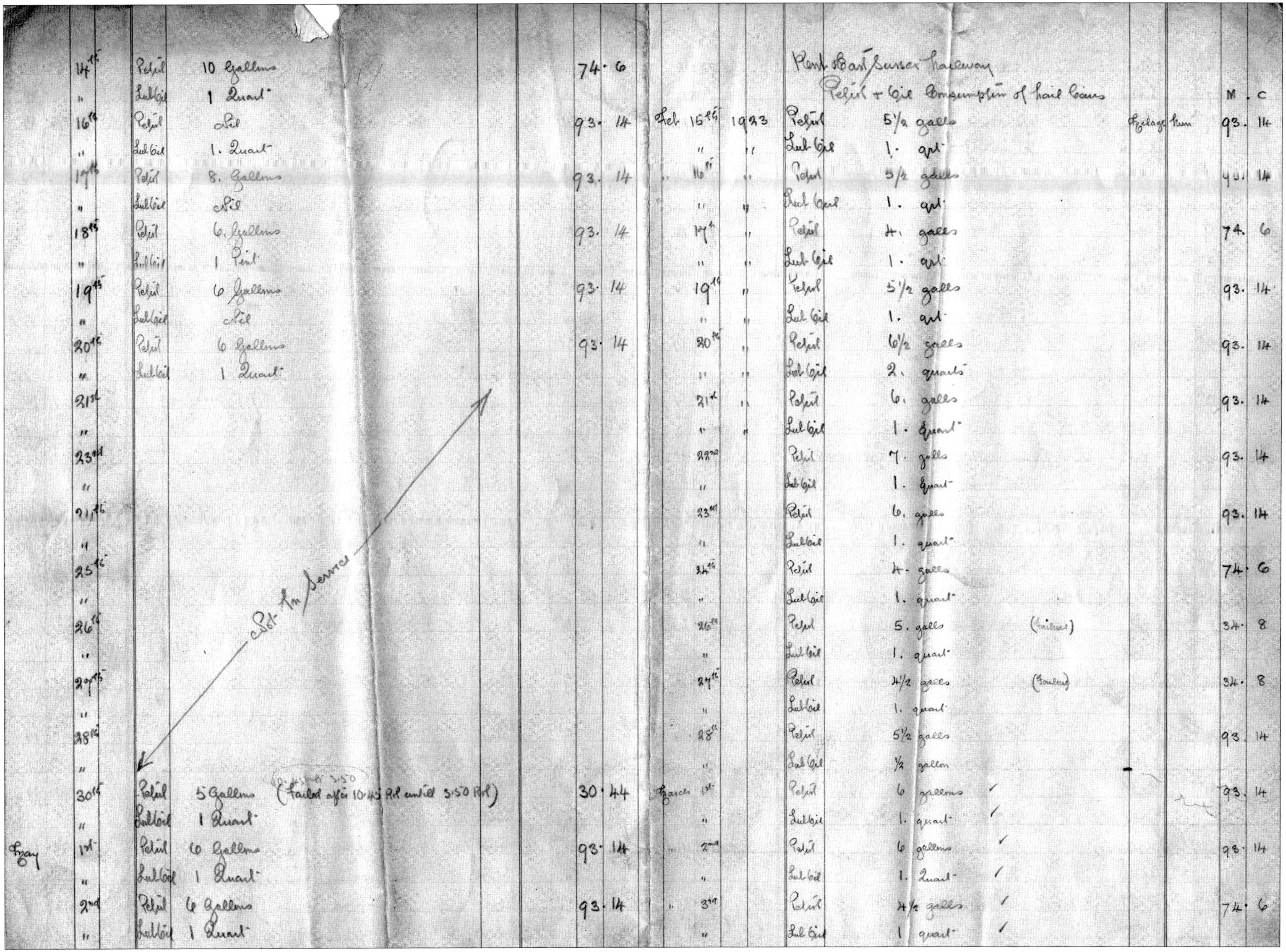

Handwritten sheets filled out by W. H. Austen as the first Ford unit is tested before entry to service.

A later photograph shows that the buffer beam has disappeared to be replaced by individual buffers at the conventional height. One of the headlights has also gone. Note the untidy arrangement of the wheel arches protruding above the running board. The radiator bonnet appears to be left open to aid cooling the engine.  *CSRM*

Driver Nelson Wood at the controls of the pioneering K&ESR Ford set in a still taken from the Pathe newsreel. Note the absence of the steering wheel from an otherwise unchanged arrangement from the road version.  *CSRM*

Clip from Pathe News film shows the first KESR railmotor leaving St. Michael's Halt on its way from Headcorn to Tenterden. The film was clearly taken from a steam engine running ahead of the railmotor.
*CSRM/Pathe*

Town to Robertsbridge Junction, returning to Headcorn at 8.13am. On leaving Headcorn at 9.51am, they reached Tenterden at 10.23am, travelling on to Robertsbridge at 10.40am, with arrival there at 11.22am. Departing at 11.40am to Tenterden, on arrival at 12.25pm, they were relieved by a steam train for the remainder of the Headcorn run. This was the end of their Saturday turn, but on weekdays, they left at 3.50pm for a Headcorn trip, arriving back at Tenterden at 5.05pm. The daily weekday mileage given for this was 93 miles 14 chains, which will have included an empty stock run from Rolvenden to Tenterden and return each day. Saturday workings omitted the Headcorn run, so totalled 74 miles 6 chains (no Sunday trains ran).

The first failures occurred on the 26th and the 27th February 1923 when, on both days, the motors could only complete the first round trip to Robertsbridge. Two weeks later, on the 14th March, a more serious in-service failure occurred, when the set failed and was unable to do the last Headcorn run. It was out of service for two days and then failed again the following day at Rolvenden on the first trip, before it could complete the run up the bank to Tenterden. It did not work at all the next day (the 19th) and, on the 21st, it did not start to run until the afternoon. Caution, and perhaps traffic levels, then dictated that it should not run over Easter (the 28th March to the 6th April) as no entries were made. Although the railmotor then resumed its normal roster, oil consumption had been rising during the latter part of May and it continued to rise, reaching some 50 per cent above previous levels. Enough was enough and the unit was taken out of service for a week, commencing the 21st April.

There might have been a myriad of reasons for individual failures, but the problems of March and April seem to have been due to the carbonising of the engines. An analysis of the lubricating oil was sought from David Kirkaldy & Sons, Testing and Experimenting Works, 99 Southwark Street, London, and a report dated the 28th May 1923, stated:

This sample is a light mineral oil of good quality though the flash point is somewhat low. It is of too low a viscosity for general use in petrol engines... and would only be suitable for those employing a splash system of lubrication. The addition of about 5% of non-drying fixed oil such as lard is desirable, tending to reduce the liability to carbonise in the cylinder.

A de-coke and change of oil seems to have done the trick. The set returned to service with one round trip on the 30th April and settled down in regular service with petrol and oil consumption reduced for the rest of its trials, the records for which terminated on the 9th June.

Stephens seemed satisfied and, in its edition dated the 14th April that year, the *Locomotive Magazine* advised:

Between Robertsbridge and Headcorn the Kent & East Sussex Ry. now convey passengers by two Ford cars placed back to back and coupled together. The original road wheels have been replaced by flanged wheels.

**Analysis of the lubricating oil used on the Ford set, ordered by Stephens from David Kirkaldy & Son, completed on the 28th May 1923.** CSRM

Colonel H. F. Stephens, the managing director of the Kent & East Sussex line, informs us that the petrol consumption for the 24 miles run, with gradients of 1 in 50, is only 1¾ gallons with a full load.

Having proved themselves, the railmotors were then used to establish a new service pattern on the railway that was shown in Bradshaw for July 1923, supplementing the existing somewhat minimalist steam services established during the First World War. In this, it now followed the classic pattern of railmotor use by increasing service frequencies in an attempt to counter competition from road-based transport. In the July timetable, the railmotors were shown as working the 9.20am train from Tenterden Town to Robertsbridge Junction, returning to Headcorn at 10.20am. On leaving Headcorn at 11.55am, they reached Tenterden at 12.35pm and travelled on to Robertsbridge at 1.20pm, with arrival at 2.10pm; returning at 2.25pm (2.45pm on Saturdays) to Tenterden. On weekdays, they then substituted, as they had during the trials, for a steam service, which left at 3.50pm for a Headcorn return trip, arriving back at 5.05pm. This finished their weekday service, but on Saturdays and Wednesdays they finished with an evening round trip to Headcorn.

This augmented service was a bold and much-needed marketing effort. Bus competition had been serious enough to warrant mention in annual reports as early as 1913. In that year, 105,000 passengers were carried; by 1919 the figure had dropped to 85,000, and to 68,000 by 1922. With the coming of the railmotors, the 1923 total train mileage leapt by nearly 25 per cent to 84,000 miles, marginally surpassing pre-war levels. The railmotors accounted for all of this and more. These high total mileages were maintained until the railway went into receivership in 1932 and services were cut to the bone. Initially, therefore, the railmotors were not used simply to cut overall running costs, but to control increased costs in the expectation of increased receipts. For the struggling Headcorn section, however, some savings were urgent and the motors continued to be used to replace obviously unremunerative steam runs.

Carrying the minor drawbacks of all pioneers, this first set was the first casualty, and it seems likely to have fallen out of use in about 1931, and was withdrawn by July 1932. One body sold on the 30th July for £1 10s (£1.50), with the remaining one sold on the 26th January 1935 for 10s (50p). Railmotor No. 1 appears to have fallen out of use around 1931, its demise possibly hastened because the gearbox of the car being towed was never completely in neutral, which caused extra wear and drag. Permission was granted from the Chancery Division to dispose of it in July 1932, Austen having described the unit as being in a very bad condition and beyond repair, but some parts thereof could be used as spare parts for the Number 2 petrol rail car set. One body from No. 1 Set Rail Cars was noted as being sold on the 30th of that month for £1 10s. 0d., but the body of the other was not disposed of to Hills until 1935, 10s for it being paid to the K&ESR on the 26th January that year.

The success of the initial railmotor on the Kent & East Sussex Railway prompted further action, and Stephens put two further Ford railmotors into service on his other lines.

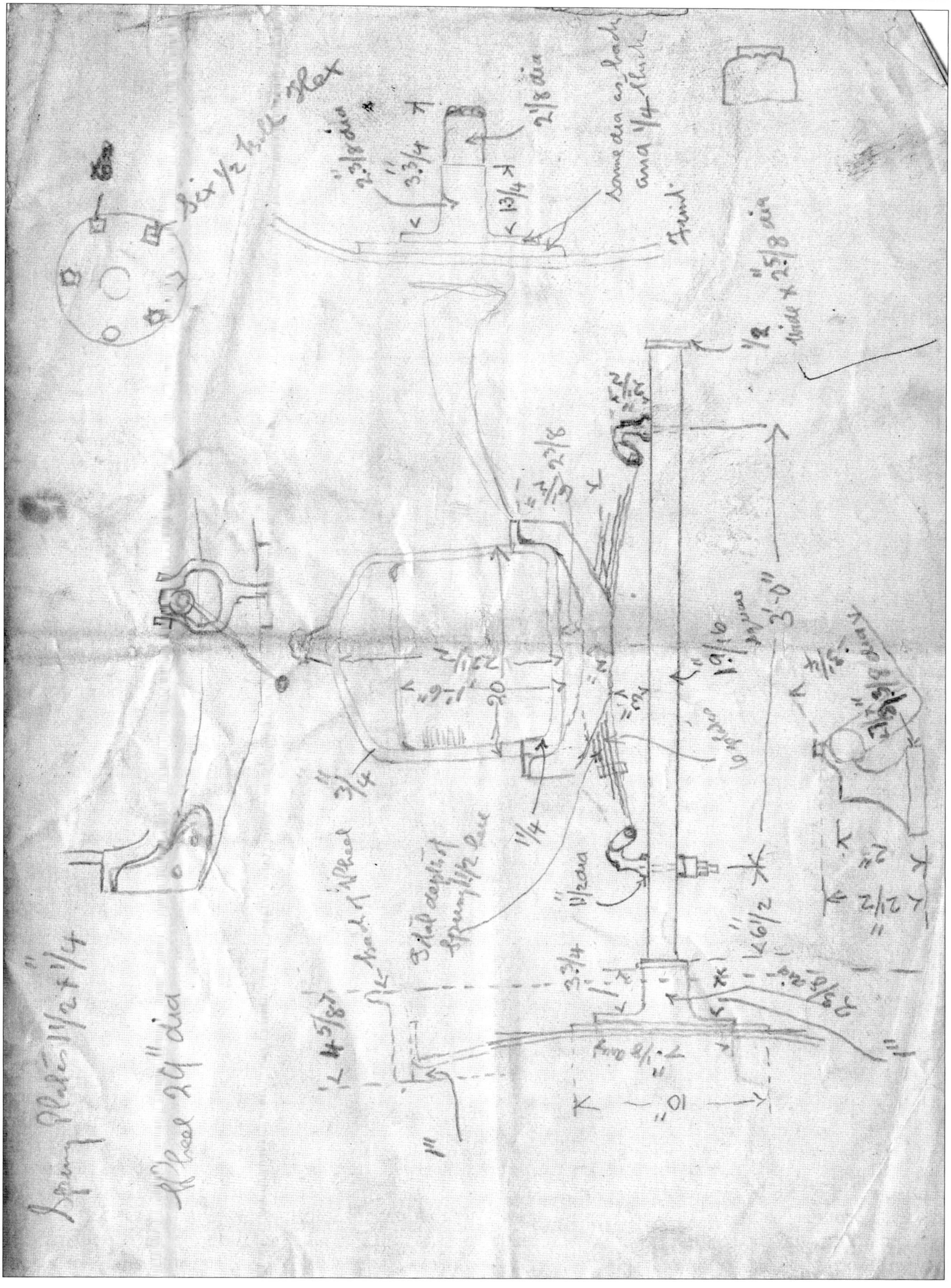

Rough notes taken by W. H. Austen sketching key dimensions of features of the Ford Railmotors.

An early view of the Shropshire & Montgomeryshire set apparently ready for inspection. Note the opening toplights, both headlights in place, disc wheels and scroll work on the luggage rails. *CSRM*

## The Shropshire and Montgomeryshire Set

In 1923, a railmotor set was introduced on the S&MR. The *Locomotive Magazine* reported the event in its issue of the 15th September 1923:

> For passenger service a three car motor train... has been put into traffic by Col H F Stephens, on the Shropshire & Montgomeryshire Railway (Shrewsbury to Llanymynech). These interesting adaptations of road motors for rail service are arranged back to back, with an intermediate dummy car in the centre, giving accommodation in all for sixty passengers. Light passenger bodies have been fitted on the motor car frames; the usual steering gear dismantled, and flanged wheels fitted to solid axles. A sliding door at the rear of each body provides access to the centre car. Centre draw pin connections are used for coupling the cars. The train maintains a good average speed, the economical rate being about 25 miles per hour, but it will run faster. It will climb gradients of 1 in 50 with 9 chains curves quite easily, and manages long stretches of 1 in 130 and 1 in 150 without overheating. It is early to give figures at present, but on trial the train ran 50 miles on 7 gallons of petrol with three cars, or working as a two-car unit just over 1½ gallons of petrol for 18 miles, the load being made up with bags of coal, etc., to the full complement of passengers. When running the gear of the rear car is placed in neutral.

Mechanically, the new set was similar to K&ESR railmotor No. 1, except that it had a Supaphord Patented Auxiliary Gear Box from new.

Overall much neater than the first Ford K&ESR railmotor, below the windows the tumblehome again curved down neatly to the full-length footboards, but this time there was no visible wheel arch for the rear wheels. The S&MR railmotor was to set the body style of both of the later sets. The centre section of the 3-piece windscreen was slightly wider than the two outer ones, each with non-opening toplights above, and the rear end was of similar design, with a central sliding door (sliding to the near-side in each case) to provide access to the other car. Of five-bay construction, the outward opening door on the front panel on either side was set back around 6in., leaving a very short window with a fixed matching toplight at the front. The front doors boasted drop windows, complete with leather strap as per mainline railway carriages, whilst all but the rear and door toplights were hinged at their bottom edge to open inwards for ventilation. The roof was of completely different design from the first set, with a simpler curved profile, white painted and covered externally with lateral and longitudinal laths, which carried a single luggage rail all round with scrollwork at the two front corners only. This construction was clearly designed to carry luggage or small packages (presumably under canvas), but in practice it never seems to have done so. There were reversible wooden slatted seats for seventeen (some say twenty) passengers in each car, one fewer per car than the first Ford, the backrests again consisted of a 4in. strip of wood attached to an iron frame that was pivoted and attached to the base of the seat. To begin with, strips of thin carpet were tied to the seats with straps, but once the straps had worn out, the carpet strips would fall on to the floor, and other uses, such as doormats, were found for them. Although an improvement on the first unit, interior lighting was minimal, with just two 6-volt 3-watt bare sidelight bulbs.

Sidelights graced the front mudguards for a short while. Soon after entering service, only one of the headlamps at either end of the unit would be serviceable at any one time, and, because no batteries were carried, the engine had to be kept revving to power the headlamps and interior lights. To hold the flimsy wooden buffing bar in place, which was positioned in front of and above the headlamps, two steel rods on either side ran up, one from under the front of the body and the other from beside the standard Ford bonnet. These were later replaced with a pair of sturdier curved metal supports of the type fitted originally to the first Ford railmotor, attached to the main chassis members below the front of the body. Small buffing blocks were soon added to the outer ends of the buffing bars, though no form of coupling was ever fitted to the outer ends of the S&MR cars.

This railmotor set was supplied with an intermediate third passenger trailer. The centre car was unique to the S&MR and it was of similar design to the power units, with matching plain disc wheels, but with an outward opening door (complete also with full drop window with its customary leather strap) positioned midway between two equal-size windows on each side. Each end bulkhead had sliding doors to match up with those of the outer cars. A footboard was provided, the length of each side, and the single luggage rail on the roof had the addition of decorative scrollwork in each of the four corners. Seating was on similar wooden slatted seats with reversible backs, but how they were arranged is not known. The complete 3-car unit was finished in unlined dark blue livery.

There are very few photographs showing the set with the trailer and it may never have run in public service, if only because of limited haulage power. If it did it, it proved shortlived because falling passenger numbers and steam stand-ins for busy market days probably rendered it redundant for normal service. The trailer remained on the books until 1930, but it ended up on the Selsey Tramway, which was showing a significant improvement in passenger numbers and was, at least, relatively flat. A visitor to the Tramway in September

**Official photograph of the Shropshire & Montgomeryshire three-car set. The middle car was quickly dispensed with, although it mysteriously appeared later on the Selsey Tramway. There appear to be no photographs of the complete set in use.** *CSRM*

This poor image is the only known photograph of the saloon on the Selsey Tramway. *David Churchill Collection*

1932, noticed a curious 'tin' saloon… *but (which) was of a build different from the railcars then in use…* parked on the back siding at Selsey in company with the Ford railmotor units, one on either side. This was the first and only positive description of the vehicle at Selsey, although a very indistinct photograph exists of the saloon standing as part of a unit on the back siding. How long the trailer remained at Selsey is not known, but it had disappeared before the Tramway closed in January 1935.

Initially, the S&MR railmotor seems to have been used to supplement the existing mixed train steam services in order to provide a better service. However, passenger numbers had been falling after the boom years of 1920-21, and with the General and coal strikes, and intense bus competition, this could not be sustained. Steam mileage fell by one half, with the railmotor mileage doubling its 1925 level by 1927. Although the published traffic statistics are a little unclear, it seems that only one mixed steam service per day remained thereafter (excluding the occasional shuttle by *Gazelle* on the Criggion Branch). The railmotor appears to have been asked to sustain three round trips daily during this period, possibly the reason the Wolseley-Siddeley and the Ford rail lorry were drafted in from the Selsey Tramway, although they were clearly of limited use. Some services were operated by one of the Fords, coupled to the rail lorry to form a short mixed train. Despite a sustained level of railmotor services from 1927 to 1929, passenger numbers were in very steep decline and fell from 50,000 in 1923 and 28,000 in 1926, to 11,000 in 1931.

An entry in the Directors' Minute Book for the 23rd September 1930 recorded that the railcars had been derailed and badly damaged, and that the line was being entirely worked by steam. A further entry on the 26th November recorded that the railcar driver had been dismissed and that the railway might dispense with railcars altogether. It is, perhaps, significant that the intermediate trailer was withdrawn during 1930; it may simply have been surplus to the line's requirements by this date. The Directors ultimately decided not to dispense with the railmotors, and

The S&MR Ford set pictured at Shrewsbury. Note the box on the running board, variously described as a tool box and petrol tank. *CSRM*

The Ford set at Criggion, the terminus of the S&MR branch from Kinnerley Junction.  *CSRM*

The S&MR set derelict in the yard at Kinnerley, showing the horn used to warn traffic at the level crossings, and the tool box cum petrol tank.
*R. G. Jarvis/CSRM*

they had returned to service by March 1931 when it was reported that they were using more petrol, even though they were running fewer services. This led to further consideration of their future and it was decided on the 29th April 1932 to discontinue their use and to dismiss the railcar driver, named as Sid Nevett. Mixed trains would operate all services from the 30th April. A falling-off in the Criggion stone traffic and a shortage of serviceable locomotives led the Directors to relent again at their meeting on the 28th November 1932, when they agreed to allow the railcars to run if necessary. Nevertheless, railmotor use was dramatically reduced in 1932 and 1933.

Regular passenger services ended on the S&MR in November 1933, but the railmotor remained available for occasional excursions and the limited services that ran on bank holidays, and they were consequently photographed on this work. A surviving train register shows that, out of the limelight, the unit was also used regularly from December 1934 on what we must assume were parcels or milk services. It operated on every weekday until January 1935 and, thereafter, on two or three days each week until early August. Mileage in 1934 and 1935 was around 2,500 each year. These runs were probably made when quarry or other traffic was insufficient to justify a steam goods working. After August 1935, operation became increasingly infrequent and railmotor mileage in 1936 dropped to 200, finally ceasing on the 30th July, although the railmotor was not officially withdrawn until 1938. *Gazelle* and her new trailer had become available to meet the need for occasional light services in June 1937, and the railmotor lay derelict. The War Department's inventory of rolling stock, dated the 5th February 1941, described both petrol coaches as unserviceable and they were broken up early in the Second World War, probably late 1941.

### Kent and East Sussex Ford Set No. 2

A second 2-car railmotor set was purchased for the K&ESR in 1924 for the price of £542 17s. 0d, paid in twelve monthly instalments of £45 4s. 9d.

The body design was identical to the S&MR motor units, though there was no intermediate passenger trailer. Mechanically, too, the new unit was apparently identical, though there was one small detailed change. In late 1923, Ford altered the pattern of the radiator so that the pressed-steel shell incorporated a large detachable lower section in which a hole was inserted to accommodate the starting handle. This, the final form of Model T radiator surround, became known as the high radiator as opposed to the

**Official photograph of the second K&ESR Ford set. Note the solid wheels and full set of headlights and sidelights. The passengers are K&ESR employees.**
*CSRM*

**A staged photograph of the interior of the second K&ESR Ford set.** *CSRM*

previous low black radiators (with the starting handle hanging somewhat precariously under the radiator) and was used on this set. Needless to say, this neat division did not survive long. One must recall that the Colonel had stated that we chose this type [Ford] as we can always get spares without delay and for no other reason. The Fords certainly had plenty of knocks and bangs that would have called for new radiators. The old low black type ultimately became standard on all the Fords. Perhaps they were available cheaply or were second-hand units. According to a memorandum to Stephens, dated the 6th November 1924, the railmotors weighed 2 tons 2cwt. each.

By 1931, the original headlamps had disappeared in favour of a single one mounted centrally above the windscreen, and a far sturdier buffer beam at axle level had replaced the original; this had a central drop-pin coupler, with coupling hooks on either side. In 1932, Charlie Turner, the company's fitter, designed attachments to the buffing beams for clearing leaves, frost or light snow. As described by Monty Baker, a long-time observer and one-time K&ESR employee:

The fitting consisted of a vertical tube with an elongated slot (for height adjustment) and contained a solid rod with a metal box at the lower end. In the box was a wire brush fastened by two wood screws through the top of the box and into the back of the brush; a set brush held the rod so that the brush just touched the rails… They were supposed to be lifted clear when not needed, but seldom were.

It should be said that such a device was not wholly novel, for the North Eastern Railway's Darlington works had fitted them to guard irons in Victorian times. They did not last long on the cash-strapped K&ESR – when it was found out that new, rather than secondhand, replacement brushes had been obtained from Webb's, the ironmongers which still operates in High Street, Tenterden, Tonbridge immediately put a stop to the practice. The metalwork remained on the buffing bars acting as very light guard irons, but was eventually knocked off by hitting the odd willow branch, or sheep or cow.

With the K&ESR going into receivership in 1932, railway services were cut to the bone and the railmotors were used – not simply to cut overall running costs, but to control spending in the expectation of increased receipts. Thus the railmotors came into their own, replacing obviously

## KENT & EAST SUSSEX RAILWAY
### FORD RAILMOTORS (2ND SET)

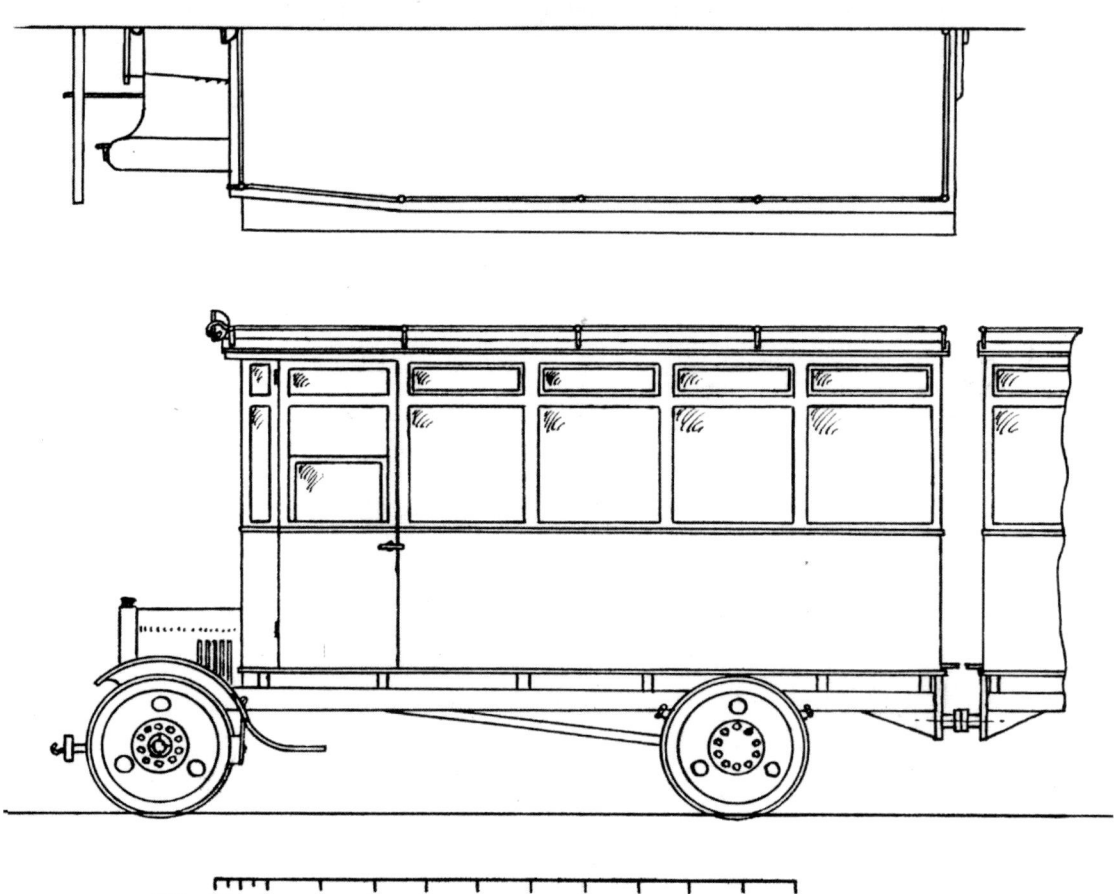

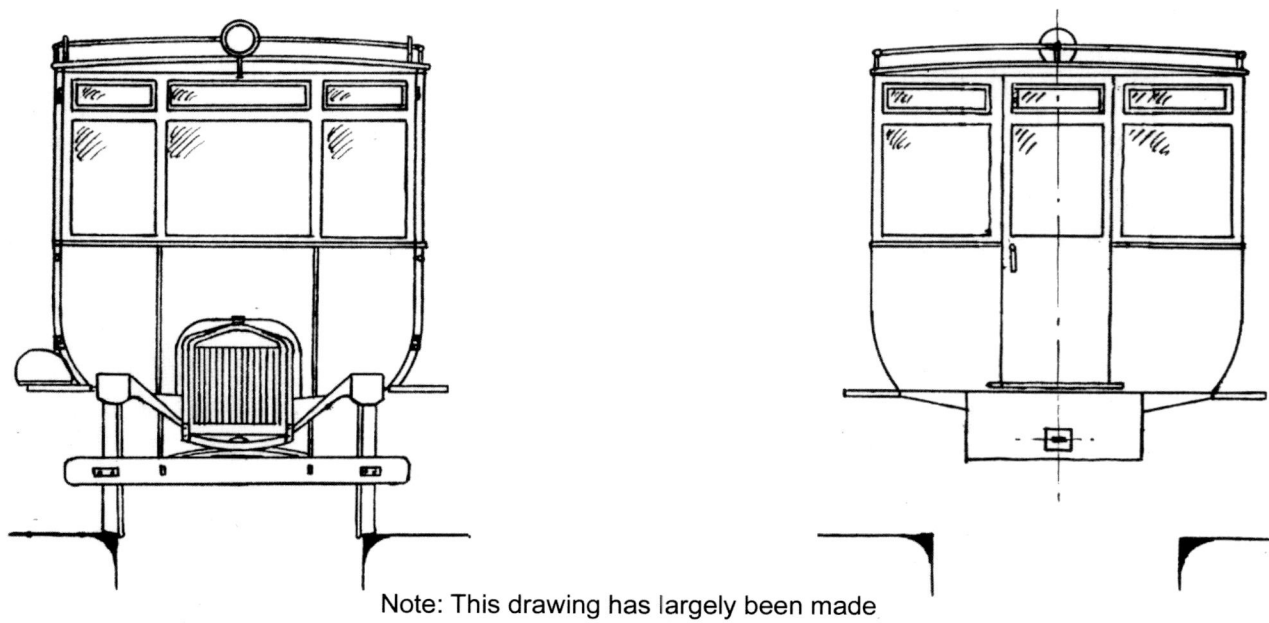

Note: This drawing has largely been made by projection from photographs, so its accuracy cannot be guaranteed.

L. Darbyshire, 2018

Taken at Headcorn the second K&ESR Ford set has a good payload. The box on the footboard is the petrol tank. Only one headlight now – relocated to the roof. *CSRM*

There is now one headlight on the second K&ESR Ford set and the buffer bar sports the coupling arrangement for towing a baggage truck. Just visible are the brackets for the track cleaning gear.
*CSRM*

# THE FORD RAILMOTORS

Waiting at Junction Road Halt on the K&ESR. Note that the buffer bar has been relocated at a higher level. The radiators needed frequent topping up with water – note also the old petrol can propped up against the radiator, ready to be used for that purpose. As ever, no luggage on the roof, but there appears to a folded canvas sheet there. *CSRM*

The second K&ESR Ford set receiving attention at Headcorn.
*CSRM*

unremunerative steam services on the struggling Tenterden to Headcorn section.

Railmotor No. 2 soldiered on until its last working day on the 27th August 1937, although the bodies were not sold until the 1st and the 8th August 1939. The chassis lingered on at Rolvenden to be sold for scrap on the 8th August 1940, along with six wagons, for a total of £62 10s. 0d.

## The Selsey Tramway Set

The Hundred of Manhood and Selsey Tramway (usually referred to as the Selsey Tramway) may have been the line on which the prototype Wolseley-Siddeley railmotor earned its living, but it was the last of Stephens' railways to have a purpose-built back-to-back set enter service. The Selsey tram, with its incredibly light track and relatively frequent services, was probably the line most affected by the introduction of railmotors. As already noted, the first one to arrive was the Wolseley-Siddeley, which entered service on Tuesday, the 11th March 1924.

K&ESR Ford railmotor No. 2 in a siding at Rolvenden. *Pope/Parkhouse Archive*

The Ford railmotor with some minor changes from the earlier models arrived early in July that year and it was to prove to be the last of Stephens' Ford railmotors. This set was photographed on the K&ESR at Tenterden, but it is uncertain why or when it was there. It might have been inadvertently delivered to that railway, or on trial there, or was in service on the K&ESR and was diverted to Selsey. We do not know.

It was different in several respects from the two previous sets, even though the K&ESR set No. 2 was apparently delivered at the same time. As with its predecessors, the standard bonnet and mudguards (complete with sidelights, although these soon disappeared) were retained, along with two headlamps and the high radiator. Instead of the predecessors pressed-steel-disc type, they were apparently cast steel, with eight curved spokes to each wheel. The bodywork was similar in overall design to the S&MR and K&ESR pairs, but beneath the windows the tumblehome was divided horizontally by a simple bead at the halfway point, which continued round and below the two front side windows. The windscreen was divided into three equal sections, with toplights above, whilst the rear end was of similar design. The livery is believed to have been plain dark chocolate-brown.

Over the years, the only visible alterations to the Selsey Ford set appear to follow the all-too-frequent road-crossing collisions, resulting in the regular replacement of the ineffective wooden buffer bars. The front curly-spoked wheels gave way, at least on the leading wheelset, to the pressed-steel-disc type, and plain panelled side doors, without beading, took the place of the originals on both cars. Although not necessarily operative at any one time, both headlamps remained in position until the end.

The introduction of this unit enabled the Tramway to provide a slight enhancement, with an extra two services each day – steam was relegated to one mixed train per day, except at peak periods. This pattern, with a reduction in winter months, continued for the rest of the line's existence. In many ways, these railmotors epitomised the Selsey in its last decade, for good or ill. Reliance on the one set backed up only with the ancient Wolseley-Siddeley and the rail lorry made for reportedly poor reliability. Consequently, it was not unknown for the railmotor to be split and operated as a single unit – a somewhat hazardous proceeding,

**The Selsey Tramway Ford set pictured on the K&ESR. It is not known why it was on the K&ESR. Was it on trial, or there for demonstration, or simply there to fill a gap going to the Selsey tramway?** *CSRM*

**Topping up the radiator with water from an old petrol can. Note the curly-spoked wheels and method of supporting the wooden buffer bar.** *CSRM*

which possibly persisted until the arrival of Stephens' Shefflex railmotor at the beginning of 1928. As the Selsey became progressively run down, the Fords seem to have become the secondary railmotor, even though apparently joined by the S&MR middle coach. They remained in service, but were recorded as poor by the Southern Railway authorities in a 1934 report.

With the closing of the Tramway in January 1935, the Ford set was dumped on the loop siding at Selsey, and, together with the railway and all its stock, it was sold to F. Watkins, a contractor of Sling, Gloucestershire, in March 1936. After the permanent way was lifted, the remaining plant, buildings and stock were sold at auction on the 30th June 1936. For some reason, the Ford chassis were cut up prior to this, and their bodies, propped up on barrels, were catalogued as lot No. 282, *'Two glass and timber saloon carriage tops'*. Their fate after the sale remains unknown.

**The Colonel's Rail Lorry**

This appears to be one car of the Selsey Tramway Ford set at Chichester getting ready for departure. Has the other car broken down? Or was it involved in one of the many level crossing accidents? It must have been hazardous running backwards. Interesting details of the platform repay study.
*CSRM*

The Ford set dumped on the loop at Selsey after the line's closure in 1935, with some freight wagons, ready for disposal.
*CSRM*

The chassis having been cut up already, the body of the Ford set was propped up on barrels and oil drums and catalogued as Lot 282 for sale by auction. *CSRM*

The lightweight railmotors were a characteristic and a much commented on feature of the Stephens' railways. However, alongside them was a noteworthy and somewhat mysterious machine - a lorry railcar – about which little is known. It might have been forgotten, but for a few photographs.

This rail lorry's origin is cloaked in obscurity. It is very clearly a Model T Ford, the lorry version of which was produced in the UK as a lightweight van from 1915 and as a stretched 1-ton variant from 1918. The latter seems to be the basis of Stephens' machine, but by the 1920s, these road vehicles were old-fashioned and inefficient, although they were freely available and cheap, and as such very likely to appeal to Stephens.

The Colonel was actively engaged in building the North Devon and Cornwall Junction Light Railway from 1922 to 1925 and, during this period, Humphrey Brandram-Jones was a young civil engineer employed on the construction of the railway, when it was nearing completion. He recorded:

Colonel Stephens visited the line several times whilst I was there. He usually arrived by road at our Hatherleigh offices in a chauffeur-driven lorry, which possessed a spare set of flanged wheels

The rail lorry and the one car from the Ford set awaiting custom at Selsey. *CSRM*

The Ford rail lorry at Llanymynech, the western terminus of the Shropshire & Montgomeryshire Railway. It is paired with a Ford passenger unit, making an economical mixed train. *CSRM*

which could be readily attached to the vehicle. By this means, he managed to visit all parts of the line where steel had been laid, in a very short time. Much of the Railway was quite remote from even the most primitive lanes and the alternative was to walk or ride the route, which was continuously submerged in a sea of mud.

With the reversing difficulties experienced in the use of the Wolseley-Siddeley on the Selsey, it seems probable that the need to find another back-to-back pair prompted Stephens to cast around and work out that his convertible lorry could be used. This odd pairing seems to have first appeared on the Selsey in April 1924, not long after the Wolseley-Siddeley had entered service.

The lorry was probably built c1919. With the windscreen being divided equally and horizontally in two, the upper section being hinged at the top to open outwards, the lorry's cab was very narrow and open-sided above the doors. The Ford bonnet and radiator grill was, of course, retained, together with its front mudguards and a single headlight, later lost. It was carried on four pressed-steel-disc wheels, but with no front buffer beam.

The expected arrival of a new railmotor set in early 1928 made the lorry and its partner redundant and they were transferred to the S&MR, probably in the autumn of 1927. As recorded above, the pair were probably used there, if intermittently. Not being particularly reliable, the lorry was nicknamed Tishy by the staff after the cartoon cross-legged race horse created by G. T. Webster for the *Daily Mail*. It was later consigned, with the Wolseley-Siddeley, to the Kinnerley dump from whence it disappeared sometime after 1932.

Stephens was a great publicist when it suited him, but he did not advertise his many low-cost palliatives. The rail lorry, therefore, served in humble obscurity before the rise in the 1930s of the investigative enthusiasts to pin its origin and use down, and it faded into the undergrowth of history.

## Other Railways

The success of the railmotors on the K&ESR prompted further action by other operators, with consideration given to use on a Welsh narrow-gauge line and a close copy put into service on the Derwent Valley Light Railway in Yorkshire, a railway with close personal connections with Stephens. These railmotors entered service on the latter line during 1924. Equipped with rather superior bodywork, they were designed to be operated singly, using small turntables when necessary. Although reportedly successful, their operation alongside goods trains on a

An unusual view of the rail lorry amongst other redundant vehicles in the yard at Kinnerley on the Shropshire & Montgomeryshire Railway, summer 1930. *H. J. Stretton Ward/Elro (R. P. Hendry collection)*

line equipped only for a single train, caused problems with the Ministry of Transport. This, combined with the arrival of a more versatile Sentinel locomotive, may have led to them falling out of regular use by 1926. Lent to the London & North Eastern Railway for passenger use during the May General Strike, they were put up for sale in June 1926, shortly before the termination, in the face of severe bus competition, of the Derwent Valley passenger service at the end of August. There is anecdotal evidence that Stephens wanted them but was outbid, and, in the event, they were sold to the County Donegal Joint Railways in Ireland. There, re-gauged, they lasted until 1934 and encouraged the production of a further Ford copy (that lasted until 1947), which pump-primed a series of very successful railcars that kept the railway open until the end of the 1950s.

The Chairman of the newly built Welsh Highland Railway, Henry Joseph Jack, was impressed with what he saw of Stephens' pioneering efforts and he wrote to G. E. Tyrwhitt, the Acting Assistant General Manager, on the 27th April 1923, to study them for use on off-peak trains. Tyrwhitt acted quickly, entering into discussions with the local Ford Dealer, Charles Hughes and Sons, and he found the proposal feasible for the 2ft gauge. Interestingly, the chassis dropped from a list price of £170 to £145 and then £115 (starter £15 extra) – a clear sign of Ford's competitiveness at this time. Hughes were aware of the Kent experience and that the Lynton Wheel & Tyre Co. had supplied the necessary flanged wheels, and a scheme, including an outline drawing, was prepared. With opening and summer services imminent, however, action lapsed, probably not helped by Tyrwhitt's return to the Great Western Railway in September. There seems, incidentally, to be no evidence that there was any proposal to move goods by flange-wheeled Ford trucks, as implied by J. I. C. Boyd in his standard history, *The Festiniog Railway* (Oakwood Press, Vol. 2, 1975 edition).

There are references in the correspondence to an earlier proposal to use Drewry railcars, after Tyrwhitt's arrival in April 1922 but before Stephens' appointment as Engineer in April 1923. One of these long-established light railcars was, of course, in action on the WC&PR at the time, but it is not certain what, if any, hand Stephens had in the original proposal. Drewry cars certainly continued to figure in the railways' planning discussions throughout 1923-24, but they were considered rather expensive and were probably not adopted for financial reasons.

The Derwent Valley Light Railway's Ford railmotor at York Layerthorpe station. Clearly more sophisticated than the Stephens railmotors, it even boasted sprung upholstery. It entered service in 1924, but passenger service on the DVLR ceased within two years of the railmotor's introduction. *CSRM*

The Derwent Valley Ford set was sold to the County Donegal Joint Railways in Ireland. Re-gauged to 3ft to suit the narrow-gauge railway, it lasted until 1934. *CSRM*

The Selsey Ford set having its radiator topped up at Chichester before setting out on another journey to Selsey c1927.

# – CHAPTER 5 –

# THE FORD RAILMOTOR EXPERIENCE

After the original novelty of the railmotors and their ability to provide a faster service than the mixed steam trains, with their frequent shunting, the railmotors did little to endear themselves to the travelling public.

A *Chichester Observer* correspondent, on Friday 30th July, 1926, was still intrigued by the internal combustion engine. Travelling to Selsey, clearly in a whimsical mood, he was apprehensive of the railmotor's state of health:

> We had only go about two miles out (bowling along at a high turn of speed), when just as I was wondering if I dare hope for a clear passage, there came a snort from the engine. At last I knew it had come. All was quiet for the next quarter of a mile and then came a series of snorts, such that only an engine worked up to the highest pitch of indignation could give, at least that was my opinion, but the driver said he didn't think it could be, he described it as 'blowing back through the carburettor'. However, I noticed that three times between Chichester and Ferry he got to argue with it, he even called for pliers, and tried to reason with it, but the engine always maintained a dignified silence until it was started. Then being so 'wound up' that it couldn't keep silent any longer, it would answer with another snort, expressive on these occasions of a lofty and noble contempt. At Ferry, however, our driver began to think that there was something more than obstinacy wrong. My private opinion is that he was seriously alarmed and feared apoplexy; so seeing a garage close by he decided to call in a 'specialist'.
>
> First of all they revived it with some water supplied out of a red petrol can. I thought at first that they might be trying to persuade [the railmotor] that it was genuine 'spirit', but I hastily discarded that idea, for I knew even our driver, who, up to now, had personally shown great personal courage, would never risk facing [the railmotor's] indignation if a dirty trick like that were played on her. Finding the water did no good, the 'specialist' got down to things. Lying flat on his back he proceeded to undo all the nuts and bolts within his reach... Our conductor, who is still quite young, gazed at him much as St. Peter must have gazed on his first vision…
>
> But to return to the business in hand. The way the man produced each article out of his inside in the correct order, each one as he wanted it, was perhaps the most marvellous of all.
>
> I must admit, however, that by this time the proceedings had begun to become a little tedious.

The Selsey Tramway Ford set 'bowling along' the Tramway embankment.

CSRM

All I wanted to do before I left was to satisfy a natural curiosity as to what was really wrong. After a most serious consultation between the 'specialists', the driver and conductor as to what could be the malady, seeing that they did not seem to be coming to any definitive conclusion, I strolled nonchalantly to the other side of the hedge from which, before making a hasty departure, I suggested it might be 'hay fever'. I immediately resumed my journey – I hate scenes.

The Selsey area always seemed to have a love hate relationship with its line. Even when new, there was some adverse comment on the new railmotor:

For twenty years (sic) a steam tram served the district faithfully and well, but such an antiquated method of conveyance was considered too slow for these hectic days, and Henry Ford came to the rescue. The result is an almost ludicrous, but none the less effective combination of ancient body and up-to-date machinery, and by means of this strange conveyance one bumps merrily along to Chichester or Selsey as the case may be. Two Ford standard one-ton trucks, engines facing opposite ways, rear axle to rear axle, compose this exceedingly strange outfit; the chassis and special four forward and reverse gear box of which were built to order. When the train arrives at a terminus the driver descends, lever in hand... and proceeds to the other driving seat ready to start again, thus obviating the necessity of shunting and tuning round. He performs his driving duties reclining in a chair similar to those seen in London parks, turning round now and then to talk to the passengers. The fact that there is a steering column but no wheel adds to the impression of comic opera transport...

Describing a trip on the Tramway towards the end of their life, and explaining just how passenger unfriendly they were, R. W. Rush wrote about how:

...he had the pleasure (?) of a journey in the Ford car and can vouch for the statement that it was an experience to be remembered. The roar of the engine, the exhaust fumes, the bumping and swaying as the car passed over the uneven track, all combined to impress the journey on the memory. The villagers, however, seemed inured to it possibly because they had learned that it was a little more comfortable to travel in the rear un-powered car!

The "exceedingly strange" combination of "two Ford standard one-ton trucks, engines facing opposite ways, rear axle to rear axle" here seen alongside the more familiar combination of ancient steam engine plus ancient carriage at Selsey c1924. *CSRM*

Passenger accommodation was generally regarded as very poor, with their uncomfortable narrow wooden seats, and passengers who were brave enough to tolerate the cold (there was no heating on the Fords) usually carried an extra item of clothing to fold up as a cushion. It was known for one driver on the K&ESR to conjure up a mat that he had hidden under his own seat for an elderly lady passenger or a particularly pretty young one. Even this basic accommodation worsened with age. On the 27th July 1931, a Mr V. R. Webster had taken a trip from Llanymynech to Kinnerley Junction on the S&MR in a 2-carriage steam-hauled train, but his return journey was made in the railmotor. He later wrote:

The timetable allowed for eventualities and said 'Kinnerley Junction depart about...' This was as well as my return train turned up some three-quarters of an hour after the 'about' time. Its arrival was heralded by the honking of a motor horn of obvious Detroit origin. It proved to be what Mr. Funnell (Kinnerley's station master) called 'the cars'... Some semblance of an effort was made by the driver to enable me to make my connection with the next Cambrian line train at Llanymynech and instead of stopping at intermediate stations he sounded the horn in a prolonged manner, slowed up, and if no one appeared, put his foot down and went on at top speed. The motion was nauseating and there was a list on the starboard side (on which I was sitting). From the sundry openings of the floor boards, where the gear levers went through, there issued a constant stream of dust, bits of grass, dead flies, dandelion 'clocks' and the like, all of which circulated freely and with surprising velocity around the inside of the car, and a goodly quantity of which I later found in my hair, pockets and turn-ups of my trousers. At one time a chicken in the four-foot way caused a severe reduction in speed, but in spite of prolonged sounding of the horn, the bird would go neither to left or right, but ran on ahead, straight as a die, and only left the track when we came to the sharp left-hand curve that brings the line into Llanymynech station.

It is interesting to note that seals for these necessary control slots producing the detritus were an optional extra from Ford, but at 7s. 6d per set, were presumably considered too much of a luxury.

Frightening as it might seem, the two units did not always work together on the Selsey line, as witnessed by Dick Cash (an East Kent Railway employee) who had been sent down to Selsey to work for a few weeks in 1926. He reported:

I had a return ride in the railbus. It ran by itself without a second one attached, and when I saw it, I wondered where on earth I had got to!

The staff had quite a time of it too, though whether the experience was worse than working on elderly steam locomotives is debatable. When railmotors were first introduced, there were few cars on the roads, and steam drivers, firemen and fitters who had to drive them had no experience of the internal (or 'infernal', as Monty Baker, who joined the K&ESR in 1923, said the staff called them) combustion engine.

A good supply of water was necessary as the vibrations on the radiators caused them to leak profusely, and the petrol cans visible on running boards in many photographs actually contained extra radiator water. Horse manure for plugging radiators was a vital part of the emergency equipment carried at all times, which also included the spanner that tightened the band drives on the gearbox of the Fords. When towing the special trucks, overheating and boiling over was a particular problem and thus extra water was vital. Whilst ample provision was made for carrying a good supply of petrol, an even greater supply of water was necessary.

Staff accounts of workings on the K&ESR Ford railmotors in their later days came from Baker:

There was no oil pump, but the sump was the flywheel casing. As the flywheel revolved, it splashed oil around the bearings, some being deposited into a small funnel on a forward sloping pipe that conveyed oil to the timing gears and the front of the engine. Ford recommended an oil consumption of 1 gallon of engine oil to 500 miles, so the levels had to be constantly checked, especially at the start of the day.

In the summer, starting the Ford was not too bad, but in winter it was horrific! There was no such thing as anti-freeze, so radiators were emptied at night, and re-filled with some warm water from a loco in steam in the shed in the morning, plus a handful of horse dung to seal the many leaks in the radiators. There was no dipstick, so the drivers crawled underneath to check the two taps on the flywheel casing, a Max level and a Min level. As the oil filler was at the front of the engine, it entailed more crawling to check when oil started dripping from the Max tap, then close it… Next job in the preparation programme was to top up the sand buckets, one each side of the driver's seat. A 1in. bore iron pipe went through the floor by each sand bucket, down to the rail near the rear driving wheels. Each pipe was topped with a funnel, and each bucket contained a tin, or a chipped enamel

The second K&ESR Ford railmotor set in the second platform at Tenterden Town, with extra petrol cans for carrying water. The gentleman with his shoe on the buffer bar is trusting his luck! *CSRM*

mug with which the driver tried to pour an equal amount of sand down each pipe, whilst controlling the hand throttle with the inside knee of his right leg.

With no self-starters, one very quickly learned that having mastered starting the thing, one did not stall it, as this meant setting up all the controls again and leaping off the platform into the four foot, ducking under the buffer beam, cranking it up and climbing up on the platform again. This was often repeated several times, with various alterations of ignition and hand throttle positions before it restarted.

On the Fords, the steering column was retained, minus the steering wheel, leaving the hand-operated advance and retard lever on the left, with the hand-throttle lever on the right. The arrangement of the gearbox and clutch of the Model T was (for its day) exceedingly ingenious and simple. The three foot pedals, all the same size, from left to right, were: clutch, reverse and footbrake.

To introduce low gear, the clutch pedal was pushed forward as far as it would go. It then tightened the contracting band on the low-gear drum by means of cams and brought this gear into operation for the purpose of climbing a steep hill, or moving away from a standstill. To introduce the high gear, the clutch pedal was allowed to come back towards

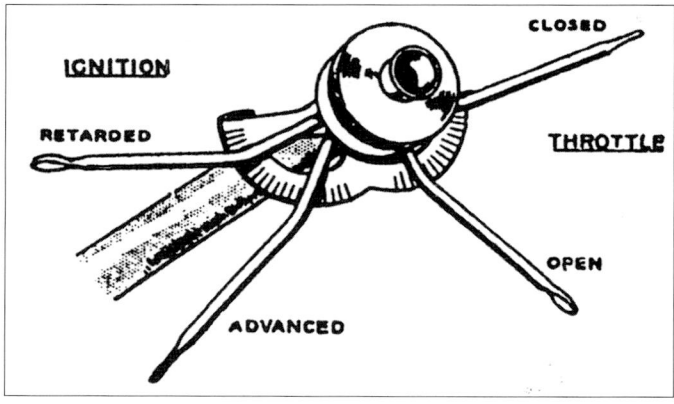

This illustration of the driving equipment on the steering column bereft of the redundant steering wheel, and the following two drawings of the pedals and the handbrake, were originally published in the *Tenterden Terrier*, the house journal of the Kent & East Sussex Railway, No. 67, Summer 1995. The name of the illustrator is not recorded.

the driver under the influence of the clutch spring. In this position, the low-gear brake-band was released, and, at the same time, the clutch discs were brought closely into contact with one another and consequently furnished the drive. Midway between the low-gear position and that in which top gear was engaged, there was an intermediate point at which the low gear was disengaged and the clutch was out of action. This was neutral and, in order to make it possible for this pedal position to be retained without the driver having to keep his foot down, a very clever interconnection was made with the handbrake lever, whereby the latter, on being pulled back, thus holding the vehicle stationary, inserted a small cam-shaped arrangement under the clutch operating mechanism.

The central pedal controlled the reverse gear, which was brought into action exactly similarly to the low forward gear. It will be obvious from the explanation that has already been given that when either of these gears was in engagement, the top gear clutch must be completely out of action. Therefore, depressing the reverse pedal, the driver must see that his handbrake lever is in such a position that the discs are disengaged. Pressing down the reverse pedal would then permit the car to travel backwards.

Without demisters or windscreen wipers, on a very frosty first trip, it was difficult for the driver to see where he was going, and it was a case of hoping that the hole he had scraped through the ice on the windscreen at one station would last long enough to see him to the next. Nevertheless, they had particular uses in a typical K&ESR winter, for, on the 2nd January 1925, when the River Rother burst its banks and flooded the railway, it was one of the railmotor sets that succeeded in resuming services the following day by wading through the floodwaters; the steam locomotives were unable to return to service until the 5th January.

Baker wrote of colder winter days:

It was a difficult job to get from Rolvenden up the bank to Tenterden on a frosty morning, or if the rail was at all damp. Remembering that only one pair of the eight wheels was powered, on many occasions slipping was so bad that the journey to Tenterden had to be abandoned and, after a phone call to George Dobell (Tenterden station agent) to notify him, and check he had no passengers waiting, the first journey of the day to Robertsbridge would start from Rolvenden.

The Tenterden bank problem was replicated on the S&MR, where Shrewsbury Abbey station was the terminus and principal station on the line with an immediate 1 in 47 gradient outwards. A driver on that line, Clifford Gill, recalled that around 1930, on Shrewsbury Market days, these railmotors would have both cars full of passengers and their shopping, so he used to get a young porter to assist in getting the railmotor moving. Shortly before leaving the

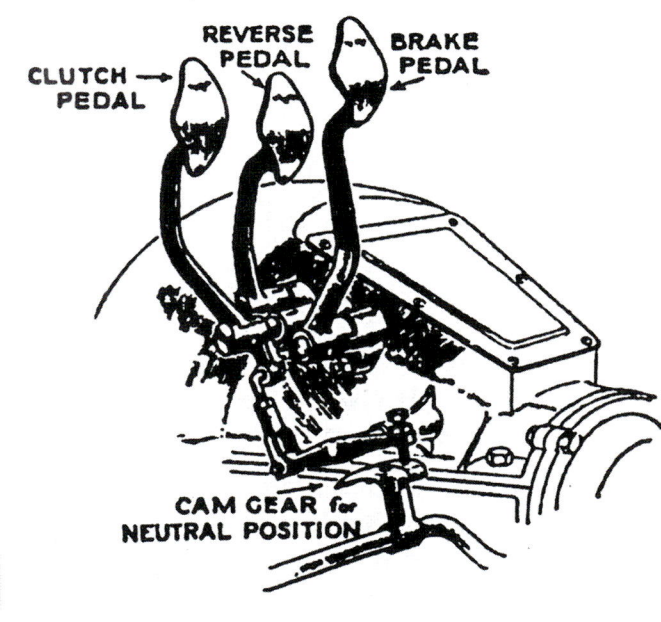

*Above*: The driver's pedals.

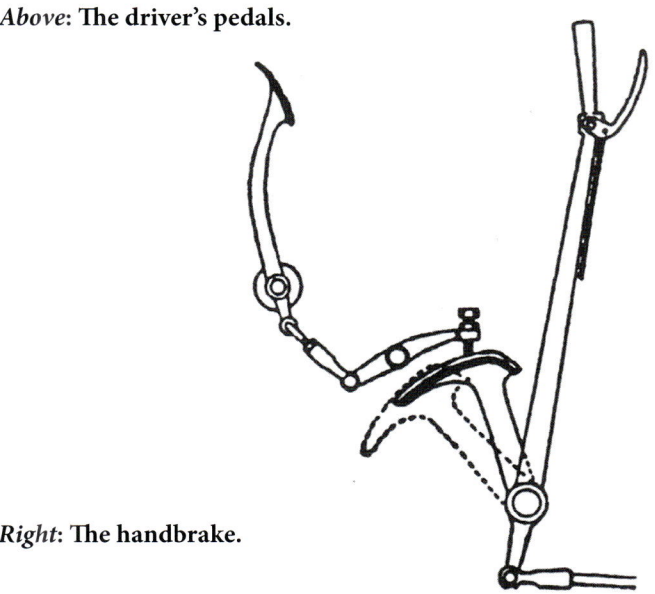

*Right*: The handbrake.

Abbey station, the porter in the rear car would start the engine, press the reverse gear pedal and open the throttle; thus both cars' engines would be working flat out up the gradient. Nearing the first station where the gradient eased off, the porter would turn off his unit, and get off at that station, presumably walking back.

Continuing in lighter vein, Baker added:

The tubular whistle was an ingenious idea, some say. It was, if you were going, for example, uphill towards Cranbrook Road Crossing (ungated in those days), in low gear and nearly full throttle, the whistle produced a sound resembling a cage of startled budgerigars. In fact, it scared all the

The driver is attending to the engine on the second Ford set at Tenterden Town. If he needs more water there are spare cans on the roof. *CSRM*

birds away for miles around! It does not take a lot of working out what happened on the downward crossing of Cranbrook Road trying to whistle with the throttle shut – nothing! This was overcome by partially applying the brake, going into neutral and opening the hand throttle, pulling the whistle lever at the same time, ready, of course, to stop if you saw any traffic coming! Many first time passengers suffered severe trauma after hearing the chirruping banshee opening up beneath their feet.

A return journey to Headcorn from Rolvenden [in a railmotor] on a hot summer's day was not unlike crossing the Sahara Desert! Towing the parcels truck meant low gear all the way to Tenterden with a change of feet pressing on the clutch pedal occasionally to prevent your legs going dead. After boiling most of the way up the bank, the radiator needed topping up for a repeat performance up St. Michael's bank, with luck making High Halden before topping up again. Crittenden bank (nearly half a mile at 1 in 50) was the only obstacle coming back, albeit a tough one, with sometimes a fill up at the summit before proceeding on to Biddenden.

In addition to the foot band brake, which was mainly used for stopping at stations, there was a wheel handbrake which applied a pair of cast iron shoes to the front pair of wheels. This was used when descending banks to save wear on the band brake. In emergency, such as suddenly being confronted by half a dozen big steers that had broken through the fence on to the track, the right hand rapidly wound the wheelbrake on, the left hand pulled the handbrake on and the right foot pushed the footbrake on after, of course, remembering to slam the hand throttle shut first!

Jack Hoad had joined the K&ESR in 1928, at the age of 14, to work under fitter Porteus and his assistant, Charlie Turner, in the workshops at Rolvenden and, apart from some part-time firing on the steam locomotives, one of his regular daily jobs was to fill up the railmotors with petrol first thing every morning. Occasionally, unofficially, he would drive the railmotors! Many years later he recalled how unreliable they were:

…we always kept a good stock of clutches and big ends, and many a time we had to have a taxi to take passengers on after a breakdown. I remember one occasion up at High Halden; Nelson Wood was driving and he suddenly saw a wheel running away in front of him and out into the fields. The axle had broken! The driver was on his own, as we didn't have guards, and he uncoupled and came straight back with the undamaged half!

It was the same on the other lines. Whilst working as an apprentice fitter on the S&MR in the late 1920s, Bill Willans would sometimes accompany Sid Nevett (the railmotor driver, who was known as Sammy) to repair the Rattlers, as he called them, when they broke down. Bill recalled:

…the scene of the disaster would, more often than not, be on the Criggion Branch, where they would pump their way on a platelayers' trolley. Failure, he remembered, usually took place in the vicinity of the Tontine Hotel, just to the south of Melverley station. Sammy Nevett did everything he could to keep the railmotor working, sometimes with the help of bits of string. At one time, he had a string around the clutch pedal to hold it out with his foot as we went along. The eastbound motor was hard to start, and I was sometimes called upon, as the only passenger for Shrewsbury in the early morning, to start it by throwing it into gear as Sammy reversed the cars from the other end.

Whatever their many faults, these lightweight railmotors were a characteristic feature of the Stephens Railway of the twenties and thirties. As a unique feature of the British railway scene, they were a pioneering and innovative effort to save costs on rural branch lines, but they have come to be seen by many as oddities. Certainly, in their latter years, this might have been the case, but, in their own way, they showed what self-contained powered railmotors could do to save money and provide a convenient service.

**The S&MR Ford railmotor at Llanymynech ready for the return journey to Kinnerley Junction.** *H. C. Casserley*

The Selsey Shefflex railmotor set pictured at Selsey in 1928. The livery is believed to have been dark chocolate-brown with intricate gold (or yellow) lining out to the front, rear and side lower panels, with a white roof. *CSRM*

# – CHAPTER 6 –

# THE SHEFFLEX RAILMOTORS

Although it was evident that the railmotors ordered from Ford were not popular with passengers, they had proved economical and reasonably reliable. Colonel Stephens was looking to expand his railmotors, and advertised for secondhand buses, presumably with a view to conversion, in *Motor Transport* magazine of the 3rd January 1927:

> **REQUIRED** 2 good second-hand motor omnibuses. Not less than 14 seaters. 4ft. 6in. – 5ft wheel track. Write Col. H F Stephens, Tonbridge.

Although we do not know what sort of response the advertisement received, Stephens moved on, and in the event turned to new vehicles. Never having been particularly fond of the Ford Model T (production of which had anyway ceased in May 1927), he sought out a new source of vehicles for his standard-gauge railways.

In December 1927, he ordered a new railmotor pair, this time from the Shefflex Motor Company of Tinsley, Sheffield. The company was an offshoot of Sheffield Simplex, established builders of luxury passenger cars, who had, during the First World War, when Commer Cars were working at full capacity to meet demands for their military trucks, been sub-contracted to manufacture lightweight 30/40 cwt. Commers. When Commer returned to normal peacetime production, the contract with the Sheffield Simplex Car Co. was ended and surplus stock was sold to R. A. Johnstone, an operator and motor dealer. Johnstone set up a production plant to build more and such lorries built at Sheffield were marketed as Shefflex. It was a low-volume business manufacturing solidly made, cheap and economical lorries sold locally. The lorry chassis chosen was,

*Above*: **Shefflex railmotor chassis, official photograph, 1928.**
*CSRM*

*Right*: **An official photograph of the engine of a Shefflex railmotor, 1928.**
*CSRM*

therefore, of a long, perhaps outdated, lineage, although production lasted until at least 1931.

## The Selsey Set

Although the initial order was credited to the Shropshire and Montgomeryshire Railway, it is doubtful if the unit was ever intended for Shropshire, as traffic there had already dropped below levels that would have made new provision necessary. Most likely, it was a misreading of a Stephens' standard letterhead, which listed all his railways. The resultant 2-car unit was sent direct to the Selsey Tramway in February 1928 and paid for by Stephens out of his own pocket, remaining his personal property.

A long article, describing this set, was published in *Locomotive Magazine* on the 15th February 1928, from which we have taken the following extracts:

**SHEFFLEX RAIL CAR. WEST SUSSEX RAILWAY**
Satisfactory results have attended the trials of a new rail car which Lieut-Col. H F Stephens has introduced on the passenger service of the West Sussex Railway (Chichester to Selsey). formerly the Hundred of Manhood and Selsey Tramway... These cars have been built by the Shefflex Motor Co. of Tinsley. Sheffield... there are two cars, each seating 23 passengers, which usually run coupled together. The wheel-base is 11ft and the overall length of the frame 16ft 8 in., plus front and rear buffers. Ball and roller bearings are used practically in every part of the chassis, while, in keeping with its place of origin, special steels are used where ordinarily mild steel would be employed.

Running empty, a steady speed of about 30 miles per hour can be maintained and the ability to pick up from very low speeds on top gear is excellent... A particularly noticeable feature of the engine is its quietness when idling. The lighting system is by CAV (by that time part of Lucas-Ed) with head and rear light, and also interior lights.

The cost of the cars for their seating accommodation of 46 passengers, is moderate, and it is the first case of this method of working, with two sets of engines being used, with English built chassis although, of course, Ford sets have been running for the last seven years on several of the associated lines dealt with through Lt-Col H. F. Stephens' office.

On the 14th December 1927, Shefflex had allotted chassis numbers 2058 and 2059 to the unit, and added 6-spoke steel flanged wheels by Wagon Repairs Ltd. Though still rather primitive vehicles by later standards, they were mechanically more sophisticated than the Fords. The engine had four cylinders of $3\frac{5}{16}$in. (100mm) bore by $4\frac{3}{5}$in. (120mm) stroke, and a 3-piece cast aluminium and tube radiator provided cooling. Petrol was gravity-fed to the Claudel carburettor from a 14-gallon tank under the driver's seat, and cooling through a three-piece cast aluminium and Dreadnought tube radiator, which was trunnion-mounted. The patent gearbox included three forward gears and one reverse, the changes being effected by a combination of sliding gears and dog clutches. As on the Fords, a gear and hand-brake locking device was fitted to prevent passengers accidentally putting these into action in the car that was being towed. Although the article suggested that a noticeable feature of the engine is its quietness when idling, witnesses found that in motion they were even noisier than the Fords. Behind the gearbox was a fabric-to-metal transmission brake, and there were fabric-faced expanding brakes acting in open drums bolted to the rear wheel spokes. Springing was better than that on the Fords, all four 6-spoke wheels being carried on semi-elliptical springs, which gave the unit a somewhat firmer and more comfortable ride.

The bodies were built by J. W. Flear Ltd, coach builders, of Burton Road, Sheffield, a company that customarily supplied the bodies for Shefflex chassis. They cost £143 each, with a further £15 for painting, varnishing and cushions. Whilst similar in general appearance to the Fords, each car was slightly longer at 16ft 8ins. over the frame (exclusive of buffers) with an 11ft wheelbase. The twenty-three seats were probably arranged with a rear-facing bench seat beside the driver and five rows of Rexine cushioned seats of the sprung throw-over type. Only some of the main window toplights opened (the centre one above the 3-piece windscreen, the front side ones ahead of the front doors and the middle of the rear three on each side), all hinged by their top edge to open outwards. The outward-opening side doors, once more fitted with drop windows and the customary leather strap, were set back behind the driver to the second bay, and heating was provided for the first time on a railmotor, with exhaust gases being ducted through hot-air pipes, which could be easily disconnected in warm weather. Although rarely, if ever, used, the single roof luggage rail was perpetuated. The original livery is believed to have been dark chocolate-brown with intricate gold (or yellow) lining out to the front, rear and side lower panels, and a white roof.

Headlights were situated on either side of the radiator and, although not present on delivery, a rear light was soon fixed under the full-length footboard on the nearside of the car facing Selsey and on the offside of that facing Chichester. A much sturdier, but shorter, buffer bar (compared with those on the Fords) was fitted to each car in front of, and in line with, the bottom of the radiator. The bar featured a drop-pin coupler with coupling hooks on either side, so that a baggage truck could be towed behind the unit as required.

When completed, the two vehicles were towed (lifted at the front) for the short journey from the factory to one of Sheffield's stations, rubber tyres having been fitted to the rear wheels. Steel flanged wheels were then substituted. The mainline railway company, understandably, refused permission for the railmotor to run to Chichester under its own power, and the two vehicles travelled on a pair of flat trucks. On the day that the railmotor arrived on the Tramway, Shefflex's representative, Mr H. G. Barton, took it for a demonstration run down the line, but when he applied the brakes with no weight on board, the rear wheels locked and the unit slid for several hundred yards over a level crossing, luckily not meeting any road vehicles. After that narrow escape, it is said that sand boxes were quickly fitted, but there is no obvious sign of such attachments in any of the known photographs. On the positive side, the Shefflex axles and wheels are said to have been

An inside view of one of the Shefflex cars. The twenty-three seats were probably arranged with a rear-facing bench seat beside the driver and five rows of Rexine cushioned seats of the sprung throw-over type. They were more comfortable than the Ford units and even had heating. September, 1928.
*CSRM*

**Detail of buffer bar showing the draw gear for towing a baggage car.** *CSRM*

much more durable in collision than those fitted to the Fords. Collision-risk remained high and, as a result, in August 1933, the set was fitted with a pair of electrically operated gongs, similar to those used on street trams, to give further warning at the numerous level crossings. Otherwise, like their Ford counterpart on the Tramway, alterations to the Shefflex set in service seem minimal.

From the arrival of the Shefflex set, the entire Selsey service, apart from one daily mixed train, was being operated by railmotors. To maintain the service, sometimes a hybrid railmotor set might be formed when a Ford would be coupled back-to-back with a Shefflex. Despite the obvious resulting economy, the introduction of a competing bus service, operated

Awaiting custom at the Chichester terminus, the Shefflex set on 26th September 1933.

The Selsey Shefflex set at Selsey with a baggage trailer in between the two units. Note the gong on the front, used to warn road traffic of the approach of the railmotor. Judging by the number of level crossing accidents it wasn't very effective.  *CSRM*

The Shefflex set with baggage trailer in use running alongside Pagham Harbour.  *CSRM*

with the latest and more comfortable buses, caused the closure of the line on the 19th January 1935. With only seven years' service to their credit, one might have expected the Shefflex set to have been transferred to the Kent & East Sussex Railway. However, operational policy there had changed following Stephens' death in 1931, with a greater use of mixed trains. Therefore, soon after the closure of the Tramway, the two chassis, with their bodies removed for a fate unknown, were towed to Chichester to be scrapped.

Selsey station with the Shefflex set awaiting custom.

The Shefflex set at Selsey with an impressive perambulator about to be loaded on the baggage trailer. *CSRM*

A Selsey hybrid railmotor consisting of a single Shefflex car and a single Ford with a baggage trailer at Bridge Halt. *CSRM*

Another picture of the Shefflex/baggage trailer/Ford hybrid combination in apparently bucolic surroundings near Bridge Halt on the Selsey Tramway. *CSRM*

Driver Nelson Wood poses next to the new K&ESR Shefflex railmotor in the loop outside Robertsbridge Junction. Note the fully opening windows. Driver Wood is clearly convinced that the Shefflex will overheat just like the Fords – he has an old petrol can of water ready. The Klaxon and its mechanism are clearly shown. *CSRM*

## The Kent & East Sussex Set

On the 5th December 1928, the K&ESR Directors asked Colonel Stephens to ascertain the cost of a new railmotor. The Board meeting in October 1929 recorded that Stephens had personally purchased a new set for £750, and it was recorded in *The Commercial Motor* of the 21st May that he had placed an order. It therefore seems probable that the second Shefflex set entered service sometime earlier in 1929. Stephens was recompensed with £938 of the company's four per cent debentures, which by that time were virtually worthless. The Shefflex Company had no gaps in its chassis number records to account for the K&ESR's railmotor pair and none of the purchasers recorded by them have any apparent connection with Stephens.

Although built by the same company, J. W. Flear, and for the same price, the body was very different from the Selsey set. The *Locomotive Magazine* dated the 14th June 1930 explained that new Ministry of Transport regulations allowed a larger body to be used on the same chassis. On the face of it, such regulations did not affect rail vehicles, but it would have altered the coachbuilder's general design, and the new body probably reflected these changed practices.

The new bodies had a white-painted domed roof without luggage rails, and the original bonnet was half recessed into the body with the dashboard, with the driver's controls moved forward 18ins. This was probably a result of changes made in that year in Shefflex's basic chassis allowing for semi-forward control. There were four windows with toplights on the front panel, two narrow ones on either side of a pair of square ones, one of which, the driver's screen, had a top-hinged opening top section and a hand-operated windscreen wiper. Front-hinged, outward-opening entrance doors, with full-drop windows and railway-style leather straps, were provided on either side of the driver. There were five windows to each side and the first two and the fourth were of the full-drop type. Above each of the windows, toplights were horizontally and centrally hinged. The sides, generously panelled with beading, curved inwards to the wide full-length wooden footboards. There were two pairs of brackets for holding destination boards on the waist panel on each side, but these appear never to have been used and soon disappeared. The design of the lower sides lends some credence to the report that these bodies were originally an order for Stafford road buses, for the curved outline of the rear mudguards can be seen. Like the sides, the rear lower panels also curved inwards, with a fixed side window on either side of a sliding door. Narrow, horizontal, wooden footboards led from the front bulkhead over

**Shefflex railmotor with baggage truck trailing at Headcorn. It has been renumbered '2', reflecting the withdrawal of the second Ford unit.** *CSRM*

# KENT & EAST SUSSEX RAILWAY
## SHEFFLEX RAILMOTORS

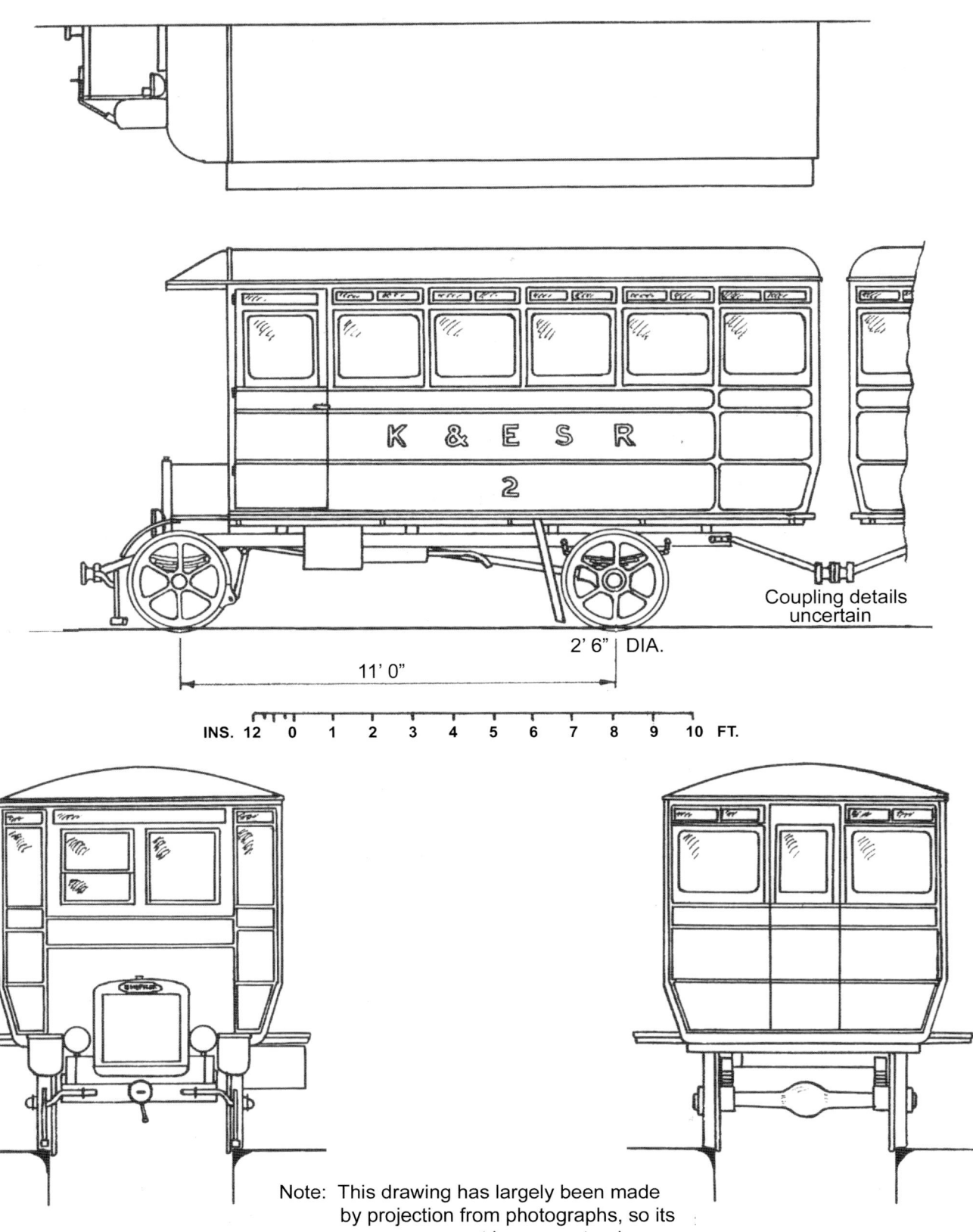

Note: This drawing has largely been made by projection from photographs, so its accuracy cannot be guaranteed.

L. Darbyshire, 2018

K&ESR Shefflex railmotor running as No. 3 at Rolvenden on its way to Robertsbridge.

The spacious new station at Headcorn Junction makes the Shefflex unit look tiny as it awaits passengers transferring from the main line. The white dome on the end of the roof shows up well. *CSRM*

the front wheels, with minimal, short, curved, metal mudguards attached to them. From the front of the chassis, two quite substantial metal bars curved down to a sturdy wooden buffing bar, slightly above axle level and just wider than the bonnet. A round, slotted, drop-pin coupling was fitted centrally and there was a coupling hook on either side. As with the second Ford set, in 1932 a pair of brushes was fixed to the front buffing bar of each car to clear leaves, frost and light snow from the rail heads. Pipes for the sandboxes were fitted in front of the rear wheels and the petrol tanks appear to have been square fittings beneath the right-hand footboard on each car. Minor changes took place in the appearance of this set over the years. The pairs of headlights were replaced by single roof-mount ones. The buffer bars were eventually removed, and the square petrol tanks below the running boards gave way to cylindrical tanks mounted above the running boards.

The driving position was slightly to the right of centre, as on the Fords, but the driver sat higher, giving him an improved view ahead. The steering column was not retained on the Shefflex; a handbrake to the rear wheels was on the left and a vertical hand-wound brake to the front wheels was on the right. A Klaxon horn was fitted, which protruded into the car body, so the push-down rod was inside. This could be operated by hand or foot, according to what was free at the time.

Seating is reported to have been for twenty-five passengers in each car on reversible back seats with cushions of a Rexine-type of oilcloth, filled with horsehair.

Probably carrying a dark-brown livery, this unit carried a number '3' centrally on the lower side panels, with 'K & E S R' in large capital letters on the panel above, probably in gold or yellow, with red shading. Sometime after 1932, it was renumbered '2', with the company's initials more widely spaced out, this time probably in plain yellow.

The Shefflexes were slightly more powerful than the Fords, but this advantage was largely cancelled out on the K&ESR by the larger, heavier body. Mechanical troubles soon loomed and in February 1930 Stephens brought in C. Milsted & Sons, Motor Engineers of West Cross, Tenterden, to make an inspection of the Shefflex railmotor, following which the company wrote to Stephens on the 20th of that month:

Re. Shefflex Rail Cars.
Our Mr Pearson went for a trip on these this morning from Tenterden to Robertsbridge to Tenterden. The chief defects noted from external and only running point of view, were as follows:-

The Shefflex enters Bodiam station. Its headlights have been removed and replaced by a single roof-mounted light. Note the hops destined for Guinness surrounding the station.
*CSRM*

The Shefflex unit is shown pulling forward from platform 2 at Tenterden Town to collect some parcels. Mind the gap! Note the petrol tank on the footboard.
*CSRM*

Awaiting the next call of duty in the goods sidings at Rolvenden. The sanding system to the rear driving wheels is clearly shown.
*CSRM*

Robertsbridge end:- New hand brake ratchet and pawl necessary.

The reversing gear needs to be held in the whole time.

The radiator leaks in the centre of a tube, obviously perished through from the inside.

There sounds to be some obvious cam shaft trouble, which cannot of course be detected without opening up the engine.

Headcorn end:- Hand brake ratchet and pawl need replacing.

The dynamo does not charge. The reason has not been investigated.

Several passengers are transferring from comfortable seats on the down London train at Robertsbridge Junction. They will experience a lively ride on the Shefflex unit, although more comfortable than the Ford railmotors.
*CSRM*

Both engines are very erratic as regards tick over [and] cannot be left set with any assurance that the engine [will keep] running.

[The rail cars] we understand are going to be in the shop [for repair] tomorrow, Friday, for cleaning and general [overhaul, when Mr. Pearson] will take the opportunity of having a closer and general examination of the chassis, letting you have a report in the post the following night.

Keeping to their word, Milsted's sent their report to Salford Terrace on the 21st February, but the original is in such poor condition, owing to the effects of damp and rain, that only a small part of it remains legible. This appears to criticise the driving and it suggests that the running of the cars could be greatly improved if the drivers were instructed rather more fully in the correct method of use of the clutch and gear box, but that quiet gear changes are rather difficult to effect. There seems little doubt that the Shefflexes required an entirely different driving technique from the simpler Fords.

Poor maintenance and a reportedly indifferent gearbox continued to give problems. At that time, inlet and exhaust valves had to be ground in by hand, new piston rings fitted every few months or so, and big end bearings had to be continually re-metalled and hand-scraped to fit. This work, and the need to fill in driving turns, led to neglect by the locomotive fitter at Rolvenden and a period of poor reliability for the whole railway. Salvation came in 1935, when an ex-Tank Corps driver, made redundant when the Selsey Tramway closed, arrived. He immediately rebuilt the set, which was back in full service within three months, thereafter working almost daily until the 8th March 1938. It then joined the Ford Railmotor in the sidings at Rolvenden and, by September 1939, the unit had been reduced to its chassis, which was finally sold for scrap on the 8th August 1940.

Notwithstanding these reliability problems, the addition of this unit made cost savings increasingly attractive, and the railmotors slowly took over from steam-hauled trains, reaching around a third of all mileage on the K&ESR, at a little short of 30,000 miles each year. Indeed, as far back as 1926, during a prolonged coal strike and the General Strike, the railmotors accounted for well over half of the services.

Despite initial success, the railmotors on the K&ESR had not been able to staunch the haemorrhage of passengers. Holding steady briefly in 1923, passenger numbers continued to decline and, although they recovered slightly in the later 1920s, they had by then reduced to half the 1919 levels. With the railway passing into receivership in 1932, the end of the experiment was in sight. Annual passenger numbers fell precipitately to 20,000, and, after a few years, the very light construction of the railmotors proved to be their downfall. As usual with internal combustion machines at that time, depreciation was rapid. As passengers deserted the railmotors for comfortable, frequent buses, and steam was needed to move the goods, railmotor mileage never again exceeded 14,000 a year.

The railmotors often lived in the lean-to next to the paint shop at Rolvenden as this picture of the Shefflex unit shows.
*CSRM*

The travel-stained Shefflex, complete with baggage truck, waits for custom at Headcorn Junction.

The end is near. The end coupling bar has gone, and the external petrol tank has been replaced with a lash-up. *CSRM*

With the bodies sold, the Shefflex chassis awaits the scrapman. *CSRM*

The Selsey Ford set has come to grief. It has collided with a lorry owned by Sadler & Co. of Westhampnett at Stockbridge level crossing on 10th June 1925. The insubstantial buffer bar and headlights have suffered most damage. Note that the front pair of curly spoked wheels had already been replaced by solid disc ones, possibly following previous collisions with road vehicles on the ungated level crossings on the line.
*CSRM*

# – CHAPTER 7 –

# INCIDENTS AND ACCIDENTS

Accidents at ungated crossings on Stephens' lines were to become rather too common, particularly with the increased motorised traffic and the coming of relatively silent (compared with steam locomotives, at least) railmotors. The Selsey Tramway was a particular sufferer, judging from the number of wheel changes and extant photos. As a contemporary reporter wrote:

Quite a number of accidents have occurred in recent years on part of the Selsey - Chichester Road crossed by the Selsey Tramway... the methods employed at the level crossings are still sadly antiquated. True, Beware of the Trains notices are displayed on either side of the crossings, but a visiting motorist, unfamiliar with the surroundings, is liable to overlook them. It may be argued that the [train] drivers always give warning of their approach by blowing the whistle, but this is not enough in these days of fast moving cars.

As road traffic increased, so did the danger of collisions on the Tramway's ungated level crossings. A particularly concealed crossing existed at Stockbridge Road in Chichester, and it was the scene of a number of accidents. Such accidents could cause heavy damage. A collision between the Shefflex set and a Southdown bus resulted in a distorted frame and fractured crankshaft. Shefflex sent one of their fitters, John Bratley, down to deal with it and the work is said to have taken six weeks to complete. A later collision with a lorry at the same crossing in 1932 left the set still coupled together but facing the line at almost 90 degrees.

The other lines had the same road-crossing problem. In early September 1926, the WC&PR's small Drewry was involved in a collision at the ungated Kingston Lane crossing. Working the 4.52pm train from Clevedon to Weston, it struck a motorcycle combination ridden by Gilbert Day, a water bailiff from Blagdon in Somerset. The combination was pushed 50 yards along the track, but, miraculously, did not overturn, nor was the driver thrown from his seat. Although the side-car was smashed, Day escaped with abrasions and shock. The passengers, on learning that he was a 'member of the working class', took up a collection for him.

Another view of the same accident. The railmotor has come up against a much more substantial road lorry. The two cars of the Ford unit have been separated by the impact and this one at least is completely off the track. *CSRM*

The Selsey Shefflex railmotor after the collision at Ferry level crossing on 20th August 1932. There is no sign of the road vehicle, but there was sufficient force to knock the front unit into the middle of the road at right angles to the track. The flimsy buffer bar has been dislodged and at least one of the front wheels appears to be buckled.  *CSRM*

Another view of the accident at Ferry level crossing in August 1932 showing the rear vehicle. It appears not to have suffered much damage, just dragged off the track onto the road. The event seems to have attracted a fair crowd of onlookers in a sparsely inhabited area.  *CSRM*

The large railmotor was prone to slipping when the brakes were applied, particularly under wet conditions. On one such day, the 3.55pm from Clevedon to Weston, a train regularly filled with schoolchildren, was approaching the gated Worle High Street crossing and a car was travelling too fast to pull up. The brakes failed to grip, and the railmotor sailed into the first crossing gate. This was not properly secured and it swung across the road, which, fortunately, was clear at the time.

Late in the evening of the 19th March 1932, a Bristol Tramways & Carriage Company coach carrying a party of rugby players, was using the Bristol Road crossing at Worle when it struck the railmotor. Two railway passengers and four in the coach were hurt. The front of the road coach was badly smashed and the driver suffered cuts and shock, but the railmotor was eventually able to continue. The railcar was derailed again that year at the same spot, on the evening of the 24th October, but it was travelling slowly, pulled up and was quickly re-railed.

One of the railcars was involved in another collision in October 1937, when it was struck by a lorry at the Bristol Road crossing at Worle. Driver Bert Woodland, who sounded his whistle when he was some distance from the crossing, thought that he was through, but the lorry collided with the back of the railmotor. Although there were apparently no serious injuries, a Mrs Wilcox of Bath, who was a passenger in the railmotor, was thrown forward in her seat and severely shaken. Soon developing paralysis and suffering hallucinations, she died a month later.

The K&ESR also suffered collisions. *The Hastings & St. Leonards Observer* reported:

Kent & East Sussex Railway fireman, Chris Robert Blair, was driving one of the railway's two Ford railmotor sets on the evening of Monday 8th April, 1929. The train was the 7.20 p.m. from Tenterden Town to Robertsbridge, and at about 7.50 p.m. it was approaching Bodiam station with a single passenger on board, Rev. Thomas Woodhouse of Brighton.

…By the light of the railmotor's 6-volt headlight, Blair saw the [white] post marking the level crossing just before Bodiam station. He blew the whistle and slowed down to about 4 m.p.h. as he approached the crossing. As he did so, he saw the headlights of a car coming down the road towards the crossing from the direction of Staplecross. He thought it was going at about 20 m.p.h., but when it was about fifteen yards from the line, it slowed down to walking speed and almost stopped. Blair assumed the car was waiting for his train to pass, and released his brake to continue into the station, but at the same time, the car driver – Clarence Wickens of Hastings – suddenly accelerated, it seemed in an attempt to get over the crossing in front of the train.

The result was predictable. The buffer beam of the railmotor struck the rear of the car. The front wheels came off the rails and the front axle broke, while all the lights went out. Fortunately, no serious injuries were reported, either on board the railmotor or to Mr Wickens and his passenger. After the accident, Mr Wickens told Blair that he had slowed down because he was familiar with the level crossing, but he had not seen the train approaching.

In a sequel to this accident, W. H. Austen took out a summons against Mr Wickens alleging that he had been driving a car in a manner dangerous to the public. He may well have been hoping to demonstrate that, as the volume of road traffic was rapidly increasing, safety at level crossings was the responsibility of road users rather than the railway company. The case was heard at Battle Petty Sessions on Tuesday the 21st May. After the court had heard Blair give his evidence, Harold Glenister, defending Mr Wickens, said that it was 'six of one and half a dozen of the other', and there was no case to answer. The magistrates agreed, and dismissed the summons.

One can be sure that this was the common conclusion to many of these incidents.

Sometimes, though, the light construction of the Ford railmotors, told against them, particularly on the light track. Local papers reported on the 12th January 1929:

A smash occurred on Wednesday afternoon on the Kent and East Sussex Light Railway, when the Ford motor-buses, which are sometimes run in the place of a steam train, jumped the rails between the Junction Halt and Robertsbridge Station, after they had just passed over the main Hastings to Hawkhurst Road.

It was the 3.24 train from Bodiam and there were two passengers, the guard, and the driver. These buses are run two together, back to back, thus one pulls on the upward journey, and the other on the return.

On reaching the place of the accident the front motor-bus seemed to jump off the rails, and ran down the bank, turning a complete somersault, the wheels preventing the second bus from following. The back of the front coach was torn out, thus uncoupling the join between the two. There was not a sound piece of glass left on the bus, and the body and metal were wrecked to such an extent that a witness of the accident afterwards said that the only description he could give was that it resembled a concertina.

The driver, who was lucky to escape with cuts and bruises, was unable to move until help was summoned, and then he crawled out, suffering badly from shock.

The two passengers, a gentleman and his wife, were thrown about when the motor-bus turned on the side of the first coach, but were otherwise unhurt, as also was the guard, who was with them.

The guard, after assisting the driver to free himself from the wreckage, started to run to Bodiam Station, but a farm labourer who was working near, and had given assistance, called and reminded him of the telephone which runs from Udiam House to Bodiam Station. The stationmaster called on the gangers, who were working near the station, and they went to the scene of the accident.

The two passengers who were catching a train at Robertsbridge Junction, were taken on the trolley, the lady at first refusing to go, but afterwards was persuaded to give way.

The line was cleared later in the evening, the first train running through to Robertsbridge about 8 o'clock.

On Thursday morning a breakdown train arrived with a crane, and lifted the last bus back on to the rails. It was found that, except for the windows being smashed, very little damage was done to the coach. The other was lifted on to the rails, where the engineers made the wheels fit to run. All of the stray pieces of metal were placed in an empty truck. The buses were taken to Rolvenden to the repairing and building sheds.

This accident seems to have taken place on the 9th January 1929 in a period of extremely cold weather; indeed, one of the most severe winters of the 20th century (there was record snow and frost, and, in early February, a great freeze that disabled a railmotor). The derailment appears to have occurred very near to Junction Road Halt, possibly at the points for the siding, where there was a low embankment that eventually led up to a bridge over the River Rother. The crew and passengers were very lucky to get off so lightly.

The service was a regular one for a railmotor at the time, and the fact that there were only two passengers on what was the busiest section of the railway shows why they were used.

The damage, as reported, was severe, and it might seem unlikely that it would have justified extensive repair. Nonetheless, repairs must have been made as, after this date, the bodywork of No. 1 looks intact, and No. 2 ran for another ten years. The fact the railmotor set must have been returned to work quickly certainly shows tremendous effort all round. The speed with which the mess was cleared up is also an object lesson in the capability of Stephens' staff. In the rapidly gathering dusk, and then the dark, the workers freed the driver, dealt with the passengers and got the trailing railmotor off the rails to clear the way.

Finally, one must cherish the image of the husband and wife passengers traveling, on a bitter January afternoon, the three miles to Robertsbridge on an open permanent way trolley. Our ancestors were made of tough stuff.

One of the vehicles of the second K&ESR railmotor stands on the siding at Bodiam built to enable the Steam Railmotor to pass normal services. The unit has lost its front axle and the workman have resourcefully used a platelayers' trolley to support the front to move it out of harm's way. The axle was probably lost in a collision with a road vehicle on the adjacent ungated level crossing. The various changes in front wheel sets demonstrate the versatility of Stephens' workforce, but might also suggest that such accidents were not unusual, if not often reported. *CSRM*

# – CHAPTER 8 –

# RAILMOTOR BAGGAGE TRUCKS

The transport of small packages and parcels and, more particularly, milk churns was a very important and regular revenue earner for all Stephens' lines. The Pickering steam railmotor made special provision for this traffic, but the coming of the internal combustion railmotors called for something more.

Although the Kent and East Sussex Railway was the first of Holman Stephens' lines to acquire a Ford railmotor, photographic evidence suggests that it was, by a long way, the last to put into service a baggage truck to go with it, for it does not appear until the Shefflex set arrived in 1929.

An undated Specification for Intermediate Goods Truck for Petrol Rail-Cars exists in the Colonel Stephens Railway Museum. It states:

'Goods truck to be substantially constructed as per enclosed blue print complete with under-carriage, springs, wheels, centre couplings and buffers combined and two safety chains with hooks at each end of truck, with side operated hand brake with brake blocks operating on one pair of wheels.

The body to be constructed of best English Seasoned Oak Solebars 4½in. x 3½in., transomes (sic) and braces 3½in. x 3½in. with one inch tongueddeal flooring, sides to be of one inch x six inch 'V' joint deal with six inch. x $^{1}/_{16}$ in. steel corner plates and 1½ in. x ¼ in. steel side battens. Centre swing loading door 3ft 0in. wide on each side, secured by means of 'T' irons and pegs.

Suitable buffers and centre couplings with safety chains and hooks to be fitted to 6in. x 3in. x 1ft 6in. C.I. substantially mounted to allow 1ft 9⅝ in. from centre of coupling to rail level.

Laminated bearing springs with shackles and axle housing to support a maximum load of 3 tons 10 cwt.

Pressed steel disc flanged wheels 29in. diameter on tread of tyre. Tyre to be not less than ⅝ in. thick on tread and 5in. wide over flange, turned to give standard railway flange and cone on tyre, fitted with cast steel hubs and floating phosphorous bronze bushes, oil lubricated with oil caps. Axles to be 2½ in. square special steel, journals to be 2in. dia. where passing through wheels, complete with collars and washers. Side action hand lever brake operating on one pair of wheels.

Truck to receive two coats of lead colour inside and outside. Outside completed with one coat of chocolate paint and one coat of varnish, including wheels and ironwork.'

We do not know when or to whom this specification was issued, or precisely what trucks were ordered, or whether the trucks we know of were ordered together. The description is that of the baggage truck found on the K&ESR after 1929, and a separate K&ESR memo, dated the 6th November 1924, exists giving a trailers weight of 1 ton 12cwt., suggesting that the specification dates from the earliest railmotor days.

The first truck of which we have hard evidence went to the Shropshire and Montgomeryshire Light Railway, its 3-plank baggage truck arriving with the Ford 3-car petrol railmotor in September 1923. Carried on similar pressed-steel wheels to those of the passenger-carrying vehicles, and mounted likewise

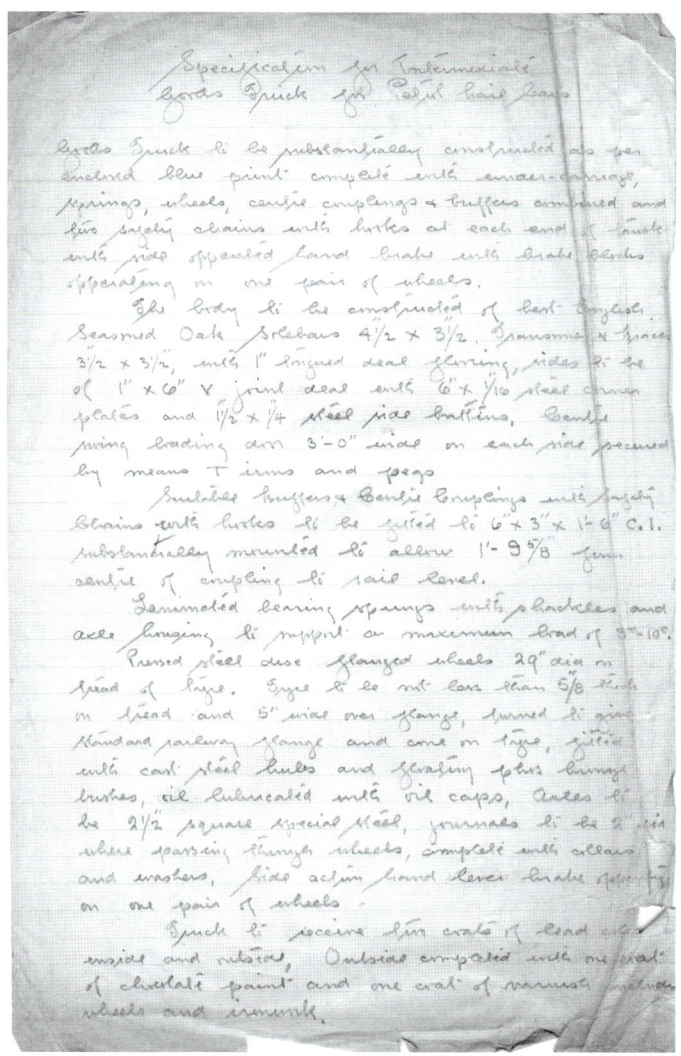

The original specification for a goods trailer in W. H. Austen's hand writing, undated. Note that it was not to be towed, but it was towed later on the K&ESR. *CSRM*

K&ESR memo dated November giving the weight of a Ford railmotor and goods truck. Given the date, this must relate to a K&ESR unit and is clear evidence that a goods trailer was present there as early as 1924. *CSRM*

on inside bearings, the truck had vertical strapping midway along the sides on either side of a centrally sited bottom-hinged opening door. Similar strapping was fixed to the right and left of the slotted square drop-pin couplings on the ends. As spares were purchased for it from Crane (Dereham) Limited over the years, it is believed that the company constructed it and, indeed, all its sisters, using Crane's own advertised pattern of pressed-steel wheels.

For the same reasons of inadequate haulage power that limited the use of the passenger trailer, the S&MR truck appears to have hardly been used, at least for its original purpose, and it disappeared from the photographic record for the next ten years. By the 1930s, it was languishing on the dump siding at Kinnerley, but, in the late 1930s, it acquired a set of small cast, and probably unsprung, buffers of the type used on the Weston, Clevedon and Portishead Light Railway truck, at the correct height for use with *Gazelle*. Again, we are not sure of its actual use. The War Department's inventory dated the 5th February 1941 noted its existence and that its solebar was bent and its undercarriage and brake gear poor, but the bottom and sides were described as fair. Clearly, it proved of use, for it was not swept away with all the other redundant stock at that time. According to a

The three-plank baggage truck arriving with the S&MR Ford 3-car petrol railmotor in September 1923. *CSMR*

In the late 1930s, the wagon acquired a set of small cast, and probably unsprung, buffers of the type used on the Weston, Clevedon and Portishead Light Railway truck, at the correct height for use with *Gazelle*. Again, we are not sure of its actual use.  *CSRM*

War Department Report dated 1948, the truck was said to have been converted to an open wagon for ashes at Kinnerley locomotive shed. It was still there, complete with its bent solebar and all of its fittings, in March 1960 when the line had finally closed, though its fate is not known. It was, thus, both the first and last of the trucks in existence.

On delivery to Chichester in 1924, the Selsey Ford set was accompanied by an open baggage truck, coupled between the two cars. Of 5-plank construction, with internal vertical strapping, it had a central bottom-hinged door to each side and was carried on four pressed-steel disc wheels with inside bearings. It was, therefore, identical to the truck that served on the K&ESR after 1929. Its life at Selsey was shortlived, ceasing at the latest, with the arrival of the Shefflex railmotor set in 1928. It is highly probable that it was the K&ESR vehicle

Photographs on the K&ESR show the truck running just with the Shefflex set and, even then, only occasionally, perhaps due to inadequate haulage power for some of the steep inclines. The second Ford set was fitted with coupling gear at about the time that the Shefflex arrived and it would have been possible for the truck to have run with this set too. When in use, this truck always seems to have been attached behind the railmotor set rather than between the cars. Later, it was adopted by the permanent way staff and it seems to have survived in departmental use

The Selsey Ford set on delivery with the goods trailer between the two vehicles. This trailer later went to the K&ESR. *CSRM*

until nationalisation. Its subsequent fate has gone unrecorded.

The K&ESR Shefflex towing the baggage trailer; the normal formation for that combination. *R. G. Jarvis/CSRM*

The K&ESR baggage trailer in departmental, static, use at Rolvenden, late 1940s. *CSRM*

**Second Selsey Goods Trailer. It was possibly used with the adjacent Shefflex set, but unlikely as it normally ran between the passenger units.**
*S. W. Baker/CSRM*

On the Selsey, by the time the Shefflex set had arrived in 1928, the truck in use was a 3-plank vehicle with external strapping and centre coupling arrangements that were identical to the S&MR truck. Where this vehicle came from and when it was built is problematic, but it was, like the Shefflex, Stephens' personal property so it was probably built for the Selsey in 1928. It was normal on the Tramway for the trucks to run between the cars, as this removed any need for shunting between trips. Outer couplings were, in any event, not provided on the Selsey Ford set. The truck was extremely well used for almost every class of traffic, ranging from prams and ice-cream carts, to small livestock and the more adventurous class of passenger in fine weather.

At the closure of the line, the truck was lined up at Chichester with the property belonging to Stephens' executors, the Shefflex set chassis and the locomotive, *Morous*. It is not clear how these were disposed of, but it is probable that they went for scrap separately from the rest of the line's stock.

**The Selsey set with the baggage trailer in between the two units waiting for custom at Selsey.**
*CSRM*

'We carry everything!' A calf being unloaded from the Selsey baggage trailer among the milk churns. *CSRM*

Boy Scouts enjoying a trip on the Selsey Tramway, August 1928. This photograph shows that the trailer was sometimes hauled on that line. *CSRM*

**W&CPR small Drewry and goods trailer showing the importance of milk traffic.** *H. G. W. Household/CSRM*

With the introduction of the first Drewry railmotor on the WC&PR, it became apparent that the addition of a trailer would enable it to handle the extensive milk-churn traffic economically. The railway had some relatively small wagons in stock, and one of these No 19, a 7ft wheelbase ex-Midland Railway 3-plank drop-side wagon, was slightly adapted for use with the railmotor. Two stanchions were attached to each side so that dropping the sides would fill the gap between loading dock and wagon to ease the transfer of the heavy churns. In spite of No. 19's small size, it proved too heavy, and a special

**WC&PR goods trailer in Clevedon yard.**  *G. Farr/CSRM*

truck was ordered instead. This was delivered from Crane's on the 21st September 1925 and was identical in most respects to the S&MR truck. It had a capacity of 3 tons 10cwt. and was fitted with a 3-plank body measuring 12ft x 7ft with sides 18in. high. There were hinged doors in the centre of each side, but these seem to be missing in most photographs. The most important difference from the other railmotor trucks was that it was necessary to raise its height to correspond to platforms and milk-loading points on the WC&PR. To achieve this, the axles and their disc wheels were attached to the body's frame by a sort of cantilevered steel sub-frame. The wagon is believed to have been fitted with a handbrake, but it is not clear what form this took. Buffer beams were provided at normal height, fitted with conventional hooks with screw couplings and small cast buffers. This wagon does not appear to have been used when the railmotor needed to haul its passenger trailer, and it would not have been required for the larger railmotor as this had a large goods compartment of its own. It seems also to have been useful for general departmental work on the line. Although evidence is lacking, it was presumably sent off to Swindon with the rest of the rolling stock when the line closed in 1940.

---

*Opposite*: Carrying the Stephens' baton into the 21st Century. The K&ESR was revived using an ex-GWR /BR railmotor W20W. This was purchased in 1966. it ran the first services on the revived line on 3rd February 1974. Now K&ESR No. 20, the railmotor awaits its passengers at Tenterden Town. It remains on the line and is currently (2018) undergoing heavy restoration.
*Brian Stephenson*

# – CHAPTER 8 –
# CONCLUSION

In the absence of authoritative data, any assessment of the railmotors must to an extent be speculative. It has been alleged that their noise, smell and jolting motion deterred passengers from travelling on them, but there are plenty of photographs showing railmotors with healthy loadings of apparently happy passengers. Such passengers would not have had to put up with the long delays suffered on the mixed locomotive-hauled trains, which paused at every station to add and detach wagons, or the rough motion of the coaches on the increasingly decrepit rails of the Stephens' railways in the 1930s.

Given the increasing economic pressures on rural railways during the railmotors' period of operation, it seems that they played a crucial part in keeping their lines going. If the mainline companies had shown more interest in the possibilities of the internal combustion railmotor, it is perfectly feasible that a further generation of railmotors would have been acquired second-hand as happened in the United States and France. With the loss of light-goods and passenger traffic to the roads, and with Stephens' death and the ensuing loss of enthusiasm and funding, his successor, W. H. Austen, tended to revert to existing, largely steam, resources. The Drewry car purchased from the Southern for the Weston, Clevedon and Portishead Light Railway shows what might have happened if more such vehicles had been available.

Colonel Stephens' railmotors are remembered as quaint and eccentric. In a slow news week, they would even get a mention in the national press under such headlines as THIS BUS RUNS ON THE WRONG LINES. However, the contemporary railway press, albeit a fairly uncritical one, made no such jokes and treated them as a serious solution to the problem of rural branch lines. Stephens was a pioneer, and he paid the price, particularly as his contemporaries on the British mainline railways, unlike those in Europe and overseas, largely ignored the economies that were possible with self-contained internal combustion units. His railmotors had their faults, but the final verdict must be that they did the job they were intended to do until the need for rural light railways effectively disappeared.

The late Colin Shutt drives his replica Ford railmotor on the Derwent Valley Light Railway in July 2013 as part of the railway's centenary celebrations. The railmotor was a star attraction there and offered rides to visitors, as seen here.

*Ross Shimmon Collection*

# – APPENDIX –
# THE REPLICA FORD RAILMOTOR

We cannot experience a ride in an original Ford railmotor from the Kent & East Sussex Railway, the Selsey Tramway or the Shropshire & Montgomeryshire Railway. However, thanks to the late Colin Shutt we can have a close look at the replica he built in 2004 in order to enter it in a competition. In 2007 he took it to the Kent & East Sussex Railway from his home in East Yorkshire to take part in the Colonel Stephens Society's annual weekend gathering. Having delivered it to the railway's engineering base at Rolvenden, Colin drove it up the bank to Tenterden so that it could give rides to members and visitors as it shuttled up and down the Pullman dock.

*Left: Just before Colin died in 2016, he gifted the railmotor to the Colonel Stephens Society and almost immediately gifted to the K&ESR Colonel Stephens Railway Museum. It was moved in June 2017 from Yorkshire to the Museum at Tenterden, where it can viewed in this purpose-built shelter*
*Ross Shimmon*

The replica railmotor in the Pullman Dock at Tenterden in May 2007, ready to give rides up and down the short siding. Note the brushes attached to the buffer bar, imitating the provision on at least one of the original Ford units.  *Brian Janes*

Climbing the bank into Tenterden station in May 2007.
*Ross Shimmon Collection*

Pictured alongside visiting locomotive L&NER 'J15' 65467 at Rolvenden in May 2015. *Ross Shimmon Collection*

Colin Shutt backs his railmotor into the Pullman Dock at Tenterden station in May 2007 ready to give rides to Colonel Stephens Society members and visitors to the K&ESR. The replica is a single unit so Colin had to look over his shoulder just as the drivers on the Selsey Tramway had to do when the usual back to back formation was not possible. *Ross Shimmon Collection*